Advanced Applications for Introduction to Pascal with Applications in Science and Engineering ____

SUSAN FINGER
Boston University

ELLEN FINGER

D.C. HEATH AND COMPANY
Lexington, Massachusetts   Toronto

to Amy, who is a joyful addition to our lives

Introduction

This book contains advanced topics that supplement topics covered in *Introduction to Pascal with Applications in Science and Engineering*. It is intended for students with a background in mathematics and an interest in using a computer to assist in solving problems. Many of the chapters in this supplement cover application topics that require an understanding of calculus and/or linear algebra. Applications 1 through 5 discuss methods of solving common problems in science and engineering using a computer. Application 1 develops the standard technique of linear interpolation. Application 2 is an introduction to discrete-time systems. Neither Application 1 nor 2 requires advanced math, but the solutions to both case studies use the record and file data structures, which are covered in Chapters 13 and 14 in the main text. Applications 3, 4, and 5 develop methods that can be used on a computer to approximate solutions to problems in calculus. The topics covered are differentiation, integration, and root finding. These applications require some familiarity with calculus. The last four applications were written to supplement specific chapters in the main text: Application 6, the quick sort, supplements the application of searching and sorting in Chapter 11. This application requires an understanding of recursion, which is covered in Chapter 15 of the main text. Applications 7, 8, and 9 are supplements to the application section on vectors and matrices in Chapter 9. These applications cover determinants, solving simultaneous equations, and matrix inversion, topics that require some familiarity with linear algebra.

The people who helped us with the main text also contributed to the supplement, and we again thank those whose names are listed in the preface to *Introduction to Pascal with Applications in Science and Engineering*. In particular, we thank Pamela Kirshen who arranged for the publication of this supplement.

S.F.
E.F.

Contents

APPLICATION **4**

Numerical Integration   40

APPLICATION **5**

Finding Roots of Equations   51

APPLICATION **6**

Quick Sort   67

APPLICATION **7**

Determinants of Matrices   77

APPLICATION 8

Solving Simultaneous Equations   89_____

APPLICATION 9

Matrix Operations   117_____

Linear Interpolation

CASE STUDY 1
Using the steam tables

In an industrial process, water is heated in a pressurized vessel until a specified temperature is reached. The vessel contains 15.0 kg of water. The water is heated in stages, and the engineer in charge would like to be able to compute the amount of additional heat required to raise the temperature at any stage by 5.0°C.

The *specific heat* of a substance is defined as the energy in calories that must be added to 1.0 g of the substance to raise its temperature 1.0°C. The specific heat of a substance is not constant. It varies with pressure and temperature. The *calorie* (cal) is a unit commonly used in thermodynamics. (The calorie used to measure the energy in food is actually a kilocalorie.) One calorie is equal to 4.186 joules.

Problems involving the heating of water arise frequently, so tables of the specific heat for many values of pressure and temperature have been created based on experimental data. Table 1.1, which has been extracted from a larger table, gives the specific heat of water from 250.0°C to 500.0°C at a pressure of 2.0 atmospheres (atm).

TABLE 1.1
Specific heat of water at a
constant pressure of 2.0 atm

Temperature (°C)	Specific Heat (cal/g/°C)
250.0	0.477
300.0	0.481
350.0	0.486
400.0	0.492
450.0	0.500
500.0	0.508

Write a program that will compute the energy in calories required to raise by 5.0°C any initial water temperature between 250.0°C and 500.0°C, inclusive.

Algorithm development

For the problem in Case Study 1, you need to compute the amount of energy required to raise a given temperature by 5.0°C, using the values in Table 1.1 for the specific heat of water. Equation 1.1 gives the formula for computing the energy required to raise the temperature by ΔT:

$$E = \Delta T m C_T \tag{1.1}$$

where E = energy in calories

   ΔT = change in temperature in degrees Celsius

   m = mass of water in grams

   C_T = specific heat of water at temperature T given in calories per gram per degree Celsius

For Equation 1.1 to be valid, the change in temperature, ΔT, must be small enough that the specific heat, C_T, is essentially constant. In order to devise an algorithm for computing the amount of energy necessary to raise the temperature by 5.0°C, you must make the following decision: Can you assume that the specific heat is essentially constant over a 5.0-degree range or must you compute it each time the water temperature rises 1.0 degree? If the specific heat is constant within the range, you can set ΔT in Equation 1.1 equal to 5.0°C to compute the energy. If the specific heat is not assumed to be constant, you must use Equation 1.1 to compute the energy required for each degree rise and then take the sum of the energies. Equation 1.2 gives the formula for computing the energy required to raise the temperature from T_1 to T_2 by 1.0-degree temperature rises. (ΔT does not appear in the equation because it is equal to 1.0.)

$$E = \sum_{T=T_1}^{T_2} m C_T \tag{1.2}$$

For the algorithm development we will use Equation 1.2 because it is valid for both large and small temperature changes. Using Equation 1.2 does, however, require more computation time because a multiplication operation must be performed for each degree rise and a running total must be kept. Programmers must often make a tradeoff between accuracy and computation time. The final decision is based on who will be using the program, whether execution time will be a critical factor, and how the results of the computation will be used.

The solution to the case study requires a function that returns the specific heat for any value of the temperature between 250.0°C and 500.0°C. If the temperature is one of the tabulated values, no computation is required. But to determine the specific heat for a temperature that lies between the tabulated values, such as 412.0°C, a method for estimating the specific heat at temperatures not given in Table 1.1 will be needed. The topic of this section will be the development of an algorithm for estimating these values. Assuming that an estimation method is developed, Algorithm 1.1 can be used to compute the energy required to raise the temperature from T_1 to T_2.

ALGORITHM 1.1   Algorithm for Case Study 1

begin algorithm

1. Set up the program
   a. Read the **SteamTable** values from a **file**
   b. Read the **Initial** and **Final** temperatures from the terminal
   c. Read the **Mass** of the water from the terminal
   d. Set the **Current** temperature to the **Initial** temperature
      Current ← Initial
   e. Set the running total for the total energy required to 0.0
      TotalEnergy ← 0.0

2. Repeat
   a. Compute the **SpecificHeat** for the **Current** temperature
   b. Compute the **Energy** required to raise the **Mass** of water 1.0 degree Celsius from the current temperature
      Energy ← Mass ∗ SpecificHeat
   c. Add **Energy** to the running total
      TotalEnergy ← TotalEnergy + Energy
   d. Increment the degrees by 1.0
      Current ← Current + 1.0
   until **Current >= Final**

3. Report the **TotalEnergy** required
end algorithm

Linear interpolation

There are several possible algorithms for approximating a value that falls between two tabulated values, such as the specific heat in the case study. One method is to round the temperature to the nearest tabulated value and return the specific heat for that value. For the specific heat at 412.0°C, use of this algorithm would yield 0.492, the tabulated value for 400.0°C.

Another approach is to average the specific heat for the two closest tabulated values. For the specific heat at 412.0°C, use of this algorithm would yield 0.496, that is, (0.492 + 0.500)/2. One obvious problem with this algorithm is that it does not take into account the fact that 412.0°C is closer to 400.0°C than to 450.0°C and therefore the specific heat for 412.0°C should be closer to the value for 400.0°C.

An improvement on the last algorithm is to take a weighted average of the two closest tabulated values, using weights proportional to the distance of the temperature from the tabulated values. This algorithm, known as *linear interpolation,* is illustrated in Figure 1.1. In Figure 1.1, x^* is a temperature

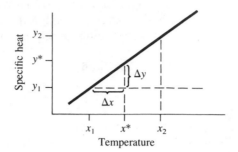

FIGURE 1.1
Linear interpolation.

that falls between the tabulated values x_1 and x_2; y^* is the specific heat at the temperature x^*.

The equation

$$\frac{\Delta x}{\Delta y} = \frac{x_2 - x_1}{y_2 - y_1} \tag{1.3}$$

follows directly from the geometry of similar triangles. Equation 1.3 can be rearranged to the following:

$$y_1 + \Delta y = \left(1 - \frac{\Delta x}{x_2 - x_1}\right)y_1 + \frac{\Delta x}{x_2 - x_1}y_2 \tag{1.4a}$$

From Figure 1.1 you can see that $y^* = y_1 - \Delta y$, so the left-hand side of Equation 1.4a can be replaced by y^* to yield an expression for the value of y^*, the specific heat at temperature x^*.

$$y^* = \left(1 - \frac{\Delta x}{x_2 - x_1}\right)y_1 + \frac{\Delta x}{x_2 - x_1}y_2 \tag{1.4b}$$

Equation 1.4b is the equation for linear interpolation. This equation can be used in the refinement of Step 2a in the algorithm for the case study, which requires that the specific heat for a given temperature be computed. Algorithm 1.2 is a general algorithm for linear interpolation, rather than a specific algorithm for the steam tables.

ALGORITHM 1.2   Algorithm for linear interpolation

begin algorithm
  1. Given the points **(X1, Y1)** and **(X2, Y2)** and **XStar,** compute **YStar**
     a. Compute **DeltaX**
         DeltaX ← XStar − X1
     b. Compute the **Ratio** that appears in both terms of Equation 14.4
         Ratio ← DeltaX / (X2 − X1)
     c. Compute **YStar** using Equation 1.4
         YStar ← (1.0 − Ratio) ∗ Y1 + Ratio ∗ Y2
end algorithm

Algorithm 1.2 can be translated into a Pascal function, with the more descriptive identifier **InterpolateY** replacing the identifier **YStar** from the algorithm:

```
function InterpolateY (XStar, X1, X2, Y1, Y2 : real ) : real;
(*      This function returns the value of Y for the point (XStar, Y)      *)
(*      which falls between the points (X1, Y1) and (X2, Y2) using         *)
(*      the formula y' = [1 - (x'-x1)/(x2-x1)]y1 + [(x'-x1)/(x2-x1)]y2.    *)

var   Ratio : real;       (* local variable to store the ratio of the sides *)
                          (* of the similar triangles. *)
      DeltaX : real;      (* local variable to store the distance between *)
                          (* X1 and XStar. *)

begin
  DeltaX := XStar - X1;
  Ratio := DeltaX / (X2 - X1);
  InterpolateY := (1.0 - Ratio) * Y1 + Ratio * Y2
end; (* function InterpolateY *)
```

To refine this function, you could ask the following questions: What happens if **X2** is less than **X1?** What happens if **XStar** is greater than **X2** which is greater than **X1?** What happens if the computed value **DeltaX** is negative? What happens if **X2** is equal to **X1?**

First, if **X2** is less than **X1,** it is as if the labels for the points (x_1, y_1) and (x_2, y_2) were exchanged in Figure 1.1 or in Equation 1.3. As long as **X1, X2, Y1,** and **Y2** are defined consistently, the algorithm is still correct.

To answer the second question, look at Figure 1.2, which illustrates the situation when **XStar** is greater than **X2** and therefore the interval Δx is larger than the distance between x_1 and x_2. Figure 1.2 is an illustration of *linear extrapolation.* In this case, the point to be estimated lies beyond the range of the known points. Although it is possible to write a function to perform linear extrapolation, the linear interpolation function should report an error when **DeltaX / (X2 − X1),** that is, **Ratio,** is greater than 1.0.

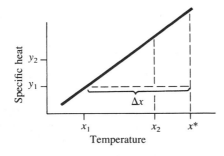

FIGURE 1.2
Δx larger than $x_2 - x_1$.

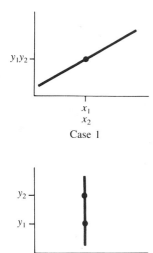

Case 1

Case 2

FIGURE 1.3
$x_1 = x_2$.

In answer to the third question, if **DeltaX** is negative, there are two possibilities: either the points have been exchanged so that (x_2, y_2) is the lower point, as discussed previously, or x^* lies below the range of the known values of x and linear extrapolation would be needed to solve for y^*. If x^* is below the range of x, **Ratio** will be negative, so the function should report an error if **Ratio** < 0.0.

Finally, if **X2** and **X1** are equal, **Ratio** will be undefined because of division by zero. Before fixing the function to avoid division by zero, ask yourself what it means if **X2** and **X1** are equal. The two situations in which **X2** and **X1** are equal are illustrated in Figure 1.3. In case 1, the value of y^* can arbitrarily be set to either y_1 or y_2 since they are equal. In case 2, the value of y^* is undetermined because it could be any value of y. Therefore, y^* can be set to either y_1 or y_2, but an error message should be generated stating that the value of the function is undetermined.

You can now modify the original function to include error checks. But before you begin to modify the function, think about where the error checks should be performed and what the error messages should say. Consider who will be using the function and who will be reading the error messages. If the function is to be used in a program that you will be running and debugging yourself, an error message such as

```
Error in InterpolateY: X1 equals X2

Current values are:   XStar =   6.0000000e01
                      (X1, Y1) = (    5.5000000e00,     0.5000000e00)
                      (X2, Y2) = (    5.5000000e00,     2.0000000e00)

InterpolateY set to Y1.  Program Continuing.
```

might be generated, since it would have meaning to you.

If, however, the function **InterpolateY** is to be used in a larger program that will be run by people who know nothing about the internal code, generating the error message above is of no use and is probably counterproductive. In a large program, more sophisticated error checking must be done, and the error message either must be more meaningful or must be suppressed. In Exercise 1 at the end of the chapter, you are asked to rewrite the function **InterpolateY** to include all of the error checking discussed above.

Solution to Case Study 1

Now that you have a function for linear interpolation, you can complete the program to compute the energy required to raise the temperature of water. One remaining problem is to set up the data structure to store the steam table. Using an array of records, you can store the entire steam table in a single data structure:

```
const MaxEntries = 100;

type   EntryRecord = record
          Temperature : real;        (* temperature in degrees.*)
          SpecificHeat : real        (* specific heat at Temperature. *)
       end; (* EntryRecord *)

       TableType = array [1..MaxEntries] of EntryRecord;

var    SteamTable : TableType;        (* array for storing the steam table. *)
```

If the entries for the steam table have been entered in a computer file created by a program that used the structure

```
var    steamfile : file of EntryRecord;
```

then values for the steam-table entries can be read from a **file** with the same structure. The procedure **SetTheTable** performs this task, reading from the **file** while **eof** is false.

```
procedure SetTheTable (var SteamT : TableType; var Num : integer);
(*      This procedure reads the steam table from the file steamfile      *)
(*      until the end of file is reached or the number of entries         *)
(*      exceeds the maximum.  The table is returned in SteamT, and        *)
(*      the number of entries read is returned in Num.                    *)
begin
  Num := 0;
  while (not eof(steamfile)) and (Num < MaxEntries) do
    begin
      Num := Num + 1;
      read (steamfile, SteamT [Num])
    end (* while *)
end; (* procedure SetTheTable *)
```

The rest of Step 1 can be implemented using the typical procedure that interactively requests data values from the user.

Step 2a of the algorithm states: Compute the **SpecificHeat** for the **Current** temperature. You know that this step requires the use of linear interpolation; however, the function **InterpolateY** that was developed requires data on the known values above and below the point of interest. So the next problem is to find the values of x_1 and x_2 that correspond to the temperatures in the steam table that the **Current** temperature falls between. That is, you need to find the value of the array index in the table such that **Current** falls between the temperature values stored at **Index** − **1** and **Index.** The function **Nearest** uses a sequential search to find the first tabulated value that is greater than **Current.** (Could a binary search have been used here? Would it have been a better solution?)

```
function Nearest (SteamT : TableType; Num : integer;
                  Current : real) : integer;
(*      Function Nearest performs a linear search of SteamT to find    *)
(*      the first tabulated value that is greater than Current.  The   *)
(*      index of the value is returned in Nearest.  If a value is not  *)
(*      found, Nearest returns a value of -1.  Num is the number of    *)
(*      entries in the table.                                          *)

var   Index : integer;        (* temporary variable for the index of the *)
                              (* value closest to Current  *)

begin
  (* The repeat-until statement searches the table until a temperature *)
  (* greater than Current is found or until there are no more entries. *)

  Index := 0;
  repeat
    Index := Index + 1
  until (SteamT [Index].Temperature > Current) or (Index >= Num);

  (* If a value is not found, Nearest must be assigned a value that *)
  (* indicates that the search was unsuccessful.  Otherwise Nearest *)
  (* is set to the index of the closest value. *)

  if Current > SteamT [Index].Temperature then
    Nearest := -1
  else
    Nearest := Index
end; (* function Nearest *)
```

Once the value of **Index** is known, the values in the steam table equivalent to (x_1, y_1) and (x_2, y_2) are known. The function **OneDegree** uses linear interpolation to return the energy required to raise the temperature 1.0° from **Current.**

```
function OneDegree (SteamT : TableType; Num : integer;
                    Current : real) : real;
(*      This function returns the energy required to raise the temp-   *)
(*      erature one degree from the Current temperature.  It uses the  *)
(*      functions InterpolateY and Nearest.  If Nearest does not file  *)
(*      an entry in the table close to Current, the specific heat is   *)
(*      set to -1.0e20.  The specific heat is the number of calories   *)
(*      required to raise 1.0 gram of a substance by 1.0 degree Celsius. *)

var   N : integer;        (* index of the nearest entry below Current. *)
      SpHeat : real;      (* specific heat at the Current temperature. *)
```

```
begin
  N := Nearest (SteamT, Num, Current);
  if (N > 1) and (N <= Num) then
    begin
      SpHeat := InterpolateY (Current,
                      SteamT [N-1].Temperature, SteamT [N-1].SpecificHeat,
                      SteamT [N].Temperature,   SteamT [N].SpecificHeat  );
      OneDegree := SpHeat
    end
  else
    OneDegree := -1.0e20
end; (* function OneDegree *)
```

The subprograms **SetTheTable, InterpolateY, Nearest,** and **OneDegree**
are included in Program 1.1, **CaloriesRequired.**

PROGRAM 1.1 Calories Required

```
program CaloriesRequired (input, output, steamfile);
(*      Program CaloriesRequired computes the energy required to        *)
(*      raise the temperature of a mass of water by a given number of   *)
(*      degrees Celsius at a pressure of 2.0 atmospheres, using the     *)
(*      specific heat table.  The specific heat table is stored in a    *)
(*      file of records.                                                *)

const MaxEntries = 100;                 (* maximum number of entries in *)
                                        (* the specific heat table.     *)

type  EntryRecord = record
         Temperature : real;
         SpecificHeat : real
      end; (* EntryRecord *)

      TableType = array [1.. MaxEntries] of EntryRecord;

var   SteamTable : TableType;

      Mass : real;                      (* mass of water in grams. *)
      InitialTemp : real;               (* initial temperature of the *)
                                        (* water in degrees Celsius. *)
      DeltaT : real;                    (* change in the temperature *)
                                        (* in degrees Celsius. *)
      steamfile : file of EntryRecord;  (* a file of records that con- *)
                                        (* tains the specific heat *)
                                        (* table. *)
      NumEntries : integer;             (* number of values in the *)
                                        (* table. *)
      Calories : real;                  (* calories required to raise *)
                                        (* the water from InitialTemp *)
                                        (* to InitialTemp + DeltaT. *)
```

```
(*$i setthetable *)
(*$i nearest *)
(*$i interpolatey *)
(*$i onedegree *)


(*$i getthedata *)
(*   procedure GetTheData (SteamT : TableType; Num : integer;               *)
(*                         var Celsius, DeltaC, HowMuch : real);            *)
(*       Procedure GetTheData reads the user-specified data on the          *)
(*       mass of the water and the initial and final temperatures.          *)
(*       The temperatures are read inside while-do loops to ensure          *)
(*       that they lie within the ranges stored in the table.               *)

  function EnergyRequired (SteamT : TableType; Num : integer;
                           Celsius, DeltaC, Grams : real) : real;
(*       Function EnergyRequired computes the energy required to raise      *)
(*       water, with a mass of Grams, at a pressure of 2.0 atmospheres      *)
(*       by DeltaC degrees from Celsius degrees.  Num is the number of      *)
(*       entries in the steam table, SteamT.                                *)

  var   DegreesSoFar : real;        (* counter for the current temperature *)
                                    (* of the water. *)
        EnergySoFar : real;         (* running total for the calories. *)
        SpHeat : real;              (* specific heat in cals/gram/degree. *)

  begin
    DegreesSoFar := Celsius;        (* set the temperature to the initial *)
                                    (* temperature of the water. *)
    EnergySoFar := 0.0;

    (* The repeat-until statement computes the energy required to raise *)
    (* one gram of water by one degree from the current temperature, adds *)
    (* the energy required to the total energy required so far, and *)
    (* increments the current temperature by one degree. *)

    repeat
      SpHeat := OneDegree (SteamT, Num, DegreesSoFar);
      EnergySoFar := EnergySoFar + SpHeat;
      DegreesSoFar := DegreesSoFar + 1.0
    until DegreesSoFar >= (Celsius + DeltaC);

    EnergyRequired := EnergySoFar * Grams
  end; (* function EnergyRequired *)


(*-----------------------------------------------------------------------*)

begin (* main program *)
  reset (steamfile);
  SetTheTable (SteamTable, NumEntries);
```

```
    GetTheData (SteamTable, NumEntries, InitialTemp, DeltaT, Mass);

    Calories := EnergyRequired (SteamTable, NumEntries, InitialTemp, DeltaT,
                        Mass);

    writeln;
    writeln (' That will require', Calories:12:1, ' calories')
end. (* program CaloriesRequired *)

=>

  This program computes the energy required to raise the
  temperature of a mass of water at a pressure of 2.0
  atmospheres by a given number of degrees

  What is the mass of the water in grams?
  □15000.0

  What is the initial temperature of the water in Celsius?
  The temperature must be between  250.0 and    500.0
  □300.0

  How many degrees Celsius do you want to raise the temperature?
  The original temperature plus the change must be less than    500.0
  □5.0

  That will require  26425037.6 calories
```

To answer the question about whether the specific heat must be computed for every degree rise of the water temperature, you could write a simpler program that computed the energy required using a constant specific heat and then compare the output of the two programs.

Problems

1. Rewrite the function **InterpolateY** to include the error checking discussed on page 6. When you rewrite the function, specify the type of user who will be reading the messages. Write a test program that invokes the function with values that cause all the errors you are testing.

2. The probability distribution for a normal random variable is tabulated in Table 1.2. Write an interactive program that uses linear interpolation to return the probability that a normal random variable is less than a given value of x.

TABLE 1.2
Tabulation of the Gaussian distribution

$$\Phi(z) = \int_{-\infty}^{z} \frac{1}{(2\pi)^{1/2}} e^{-x^2/2} \, dx = P(Z < z)$$

z	$\Phi(z)$	z	$\Phi(z)$	z	$\Phi(z)$	z	$\Phi(z)$
0.0	0.5000	1.0	0.8413	2.0	0.9772	3.0	0.9986
0.1	0.5398	1.1	0.8643	2.1	0.9821	3.1	0.9990
0.2	0.5793	1.2	0.8849	2.2	0.9861	3.2	0.9993
0.3	0.6179	1.3	0.9032	2.3	0.9893	3.3	0.9995
0.4	0.6554	1.4	0.9192	2.4	0.9918	3.4	0.9997
0.5	0.6915	1.5	0.9332	2.5	0.9938	3.5	0.99977
0.6	0.7257	1.6	0.9452	2.6	0.9953	3.6	0.99984
0.7	0.7580	1.7	0.9554	2.7	0.9965	3.7	0.99989
0.8	0.7881	1.8	0.9641	2.8	0.9974	3.8	0.99993
0.9	0.8159	1.9	0.9713	2.9	0.9981	3.9	0.99995

3. Write a program to compute the error caused by using linear interpolation to approximate the sine function. Compute values of sin (x) between $-\pi$ and π using the points sin $(x - \Delta x)$ and sin $(x + \Delta x)$ for different values of Δx. For each value of x use the true value, sin (x), to compute the error.

APPLICATION 2
Discrete-Time Systems

This application uses **files** and the random number generator that was developed in the previous section.

Time is usually thought of as a continuous quantity and represented by real numbers. In many systems, however, events can occur or can be observed only at *discrete* time periods, such as every year, month, day, hour, second, or nanosecond. In describing and analyzing events of this type, it is convenient to define time as a discrete, integer variable. In this section, techniques for modeling discrete-time systems will be covered.

CASE STUDY 2
Simulating the roll angle of a rocket

A rocket that is to be sent into space will transmit information on its current status back to earth in a stream of data. Among the variables that will be transmitted are the rocket's angular velocity, ω, and its roll angle, ϕ. Each of these variables will be transmitted once every second.

The angular velocity is the velocity at which the rocket spins around its long axis, and the roll angle is the angle through which the rocket has rotated based on an arbitrary starting position, as illustrated in Figure 2.1.

If the rocket is rolling, damping forces will slow the angular velocity until it returns to zero. However, the rocket is subject to random disturbances that cause sudden changes in the angular velocity.

At any given second, the angular velocity depends on the angular velocity in the previous second, the damping forces on the angular velocity, and the change in angular velocity due to random disturbances. Thus if the angular velocity and the change in angular velocity for the current time step are known, the angular velocity for the next time step can be computed. Similarly, the roll angle depends on the roll angle in the previous second and the change in position due to the angular velocity. So if the roll angle and the angular velocity for the current time step are known, the roll angle for the next time step can be computed.

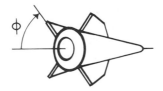

FIGURE 2.1
Roll angle, ϕ, of a rocket.

13

Before the rocket is sent up, the space agency would like to be able to predict how often the rocket's angular velocity will become so large that corrective action will have to be taken. Write a program that computes the angular velocity and roll angle of a rocket as a function of time, when the rocket is subjected to random forces. The output of the program should be equivalent to the data that will actually be transmitted by the rocket; that is, the program should *simulate* the data that will be transmitted by the rocket.

It has been decided that while the program is under development the roll angle and angular velocity will be reported every second for 6000 seconds. It has also been decided that, in order to make debugging easier, a separate program will generate the 6000 values for the random disturbances, known as noise, and store them in a computer file so that the test runs all have the same input. Because the output of the test program is 12,000 numbers, the output also will be written to a file so that it can be analyzed by other programs.

Algorithm development

A key attribute of the problem in the case study is that the values of the angular velocity and the roll angle depend only on the values in the previous time step. This attribute has implications both for the data structure and for the method of solution.

First, looking at the data structure for the case study, you can see that one way to structure the data is to use **array**s, dimensioned at 6000, to store the angular velocity and the roll angle. However, since the current time step depends only on the previous time step, only the previous and current values need to be stored at any given time. The computed values for the current time step can be written to a **file** and then saved in a computer file for future analysis.

To make writing the **file** easier and to make storing the data on each time step easier, you can organize the roll angle and angular velocity in a **record.**

```
type   TimeRec = record
          AngularVelocity : real;          (* angular velocity in radians/sec. *)
          RollAngle : real                 (* angular displacement in radians. *)
       end; (* TimeRec *)

var    LastTime : TimeRec;                  (* data for the last time step. *)
       ThisTime : TimeRec;                  (* data for the current time step. *)
       timefile : file of TimeRec;          (* output file of the data on each *)
                                            (* time step. *)
```

After including the **file** of real numbers for the input data on the random disturbances, a constant for the number of time steps, and a counter to keep track of the time step, the data structure for the problem is as follows:

```
const MaxStep = 6000;                (* maximum number of time steps. *)

type   TimeRec = record
           AngularVelocity : real;   (* angular velocity in radians/sec. *)
           RollAngle : real          (* angular displacement in radians. *)
       end; (* TimeRec *)

var    LastTime : TimeRec;           (* data for the last time step. *)
       ThisTime : TimeRec;           (* data for the current time step. *)
       Step : integer;               (* counter for the time step number. *)
       Noise : real;                 (* random disturbance in the current *)
                                     (* time period. *)
       timefile : file of TimeRec;   (* output file of the data on each *)
                                     (* time step. *)
       randomfile : file of real;    (* input file of data for the random *)
                                     (* disturbance in each time period. *)
```

To make it easier to begin writing the algorithm for the case study, we will temporarily simplify the problem by assuming that there are no random disturbances and that the angular velocity is constant. The simplified problem can be restated as follows: Given the initial position and angular velocity of the rocket, compute the roll angle of the rocket rolling with constant angular velocity. Report the roll angle every second for 6000 seconds.

Simplifying the problem statement allows you to focus on designing the structure for looping through the time steps. Because the problem definition says that the program is to be run for 6000 time steps, a **for** statement is the obvious choice. But **for** loops are not very flexible, and it was implied in the problem definition that the program will eventually be run until the upper limit for angular velocity is exceeded. To make the program more adaptable, you can use a **while-do** or a **repeat-until** loop.

Each time through the loop, the roll angle must be computed and reported. When the time step is incremented, the roll angle for what was the current time step becomes the roll angle for the previous time step. If the data were stored in **array**s, it would be possible to refer to time step k and time step $k - 1$. But because only the data on the current and the previous time step are stored, it is necessary to set the last time step equal to the current time step at the end of the loop. An algorithm for the simplified problem is as follows:

ALGORITHM 2.1   First iteration of an algorithm for the simplified case study with constant angular velocity

begin algorithm
    1. Initialize the program
        a. Set **LastTime.RollAngle** to its value for time step 0
        b. Set the angular velocity to its given value
        c. Initialize **Step**, the time counter, to 0

2. Repeat
   a. **Step ← Step** + 1
   b. Compute **ThisTime.RollAngle** based on **LastTime.RollAngle** and the constant angular velocity
   c. Report **ThisTime.RollAngle**
   d. **LastTime.RollAngle** := **ThisTime.RollAngle**
   until **Step** > 6000
end algorithm

Step 2b is the only step that needs further refinement. Knowing that there is enough information to compute the roll angle, you can leave this step at its current level of refinement and continue with the algorithm development.

The next level of the problem is to include the damping effect that causes the angular velocity to decay to zero over time. You know that at any time k, the angular velocity is a function of the original angular velocity and of the time that has elapsed, and you know that the roll angle at time k is a function of the angular velocity and elapsed time. The algorithm can be written:

ALGORITHM 2.2   Second iteration of an algorithm for the simplified case study with angular velocity damping

begin algorithm
   1. Initialize the program
      a. Set **LastTime.RollAngle** to its value for time step 0
      b. Set **LastTime.AngularVelocity** to its value for time step 0
      c. Initialize **Step,** the time counter, to 0

   2. Repeat
      a. **Step ← Step** + 1
      b. Compute **ThisTime.RollAngle,** based on **LastTime.RollAngle** and **LastTime.AngularVelocity**
      c. Compute **ThisTime.AngularVelocity** based on **LastTime.AngularVelocity** and the damping equation
      d. Report **ThisTime.AngularVelocity** and **ThisTime.RollAngle**
      e. **LastTime ← ThisTime**
      until **Step** > 6000
end algorithm

Comparing Algorithm 2.1 to Algorithm 2.2, you can see that the differences between them are due to the fact that the angular velocity is no longer assumed to be constant in Algorithm 2.2. Thus in Algorithm 2.2 the angular velocity must be computed and reported (Steps 2c and 2d) for each time step and the current value must be saved at the end of each time step (Step 2e).

Finally, you can add the random disturbances to the algorithm. For the overall structure, you only need to know that the angular velocity depends on the random disturbances in each time step. In the problem statement for Case Study 2, it was stated that the values for the random noise were stored in a computer file. Calling the associated Pascal **file randomfile,** you can write the final outline as follows:

ALGORITHM 2.3 Final iteration for an algorithm for the case study including angular velocity, damping, and random disturbances

begin algorithm

1. Initialize the program
   a. Set **LastTime.RollAngle** to its value for time step 0
   b. Set **LastTime.AngularVelocity** to its value for time step 0
   c. Initialize **Step,** the time counter, to 0

2. Repeat
   a. **Step ← Step + 1**
   b. Compute **ThisTime.RollAngle** based on **LastTime.RollAngle** and **LastTime.AngularVelocity**
   c. Read **Noise** from **randomfile**
   d. Compute the **ThisTime.AngularVelocity** based on **LastTime.AngularVelocity, Noise,** and the damping equation
   e. Report **ThisTime.AngularVelocity** and **ThisTime.RollAngle**
   f. **LastTime ← ThisTime**
   until **Step > 6000**

end algorithm

From the outline and the data structure, the main body of the Pascal program to simulate the rocket can be written

```
begin
  Initialize (Step, LastTime);
  repeat
    Step := Step + 1;

    ComputeRollAngle (Step, LastTime, ThisTime);

    ReadRandom (Noise);
    ComputeAngularVelocity (Step, Noise, LastTime, ThisTime);

    ReportThisTime (ThisTime);

    LastTime := ThisTime
  until Step > MaxStep
```

The procedures to compute the roll angle and angular velocity will be developed in the next section on discrete-time systems.

Discrete-time systems

To distinguish between continuous and discrete time, continuous time will be represented by the variable t and discrete time will be represented by the variable k.

Difference equations

An equation of the form

$$y(k) = ay(k - 1) \tag{2.1}$$

is a *difference equation*. A difference equation defines a variable in the system at time increment k in terms of the variable at a different time increment. Usually, the function $y(k)$ is defined in terms of time increments one or two time steps before or after k. For example, without the random disturbances, the angular velocity at time k is a linear function of the angular velocity at time $k - 1$:

$$v(k) = \left(1 - \frac{1}{\tau}\right)v(k - 1) \tag{2.2}$$

where τ = roll-time constant. The roll-time constant is a measure of how quickly the angular velocity is damped to zero after the rocket starts rolling.

The general form for a linear difference equation with constant coefficients is

$$a_n y(k - n) + a_{n-1}y(k - n + 1) + \cdots + a_1 y(k - 1) + a_0 y(k) = g(k) \tag{2.3}$$

A difference equation is *linear* if the terms $y(k)$ are all to the first power—that is, there are no terms like $y^2(3)$ or $\ln[y(22)]$. The coefficients a_n of a *constant-coefficient difference equation* are constants that do not depend on the time increment k. The *order* of a difference equation is the difference between the largest and the smallest time arguments of y. For example,

$$v(k) - \left(1 - \frac{1}{\tau}\right)v(k - 1) = 0 \tag{2.4}$$

is a linear, constant-coefficient difference equation of order 1. The order is 1 because the difference between the largest and smallest time arguments is $k - (k - 1) = 1$. The equation

$$y(k + 1) + 3y(k) - 2y(k - 1) = 0 \tag{2.5}$$

is a linear, constant-coefficient difference equation of order 2 because $k + 1 - (k - 1) = 2$.

A difference equation is *homogeneous* if $g(k)$, the right-hand side, is equal to zero. Equations 2.4 and 2.5 are both homogeneous.

This discussion will be limited to difference equations that are *linear*, (that is, those equations that have constant coefficients) and that are of order 1 or 2. Initially, only homogeneous equations will be considered.

Solving difference equations

A *closed-form solution* to a difference equation is an explicit expression for the function $y(k)$ in terms of k; that is, if you can write a function for $y(k)$ that only depends on k, and not on any terms like $y(k - 1)$, you have a closed-form solution for $y(k)$. Consider Equation 2.4:

$$v(k) - \left(1 - \frac{1}{\tau}\right)v(k - 1) = 0$$

In solving this equation, you are looking not for a number but for a function $v(k)$ that satisfies the equation for every value of k. Without more information, this equation cannot be solved. For most difference equations, the additional information takes the form of *initial*, or *boundary*, *conditions* in which the value of $v(k)$ is given as a constant for a particular value of k. An initial condition takes the form

$$v(0) = v_0 \qquad (2.6)$$

where v_0 is a constant equal to the initial angular velocity. Now there are two equations and two unknowns:

$$v(k) - \left(1 - \frac{1}{\tau}\right)v(k - 1) = 0$$

$$v(0) = v_0 \qquad (2.7)$$

Equation 2.7 gives the relationship between $v(k)$ and $v(k - 1)$. Each value of k does not have a separate equation. There are several techniques for solving sets of equations like Equation 2.7.

Characteristic Equations. The *characteristic* equation of a homogeneous, constant coefficient, linear difference equation can be used to find an explicit, or closed form, solution for a difference equation.

The difference equation Equation 2.4,

$$v(k) - \left(1 - \frac{1}{\tau}\right)v(k - 1) = 0$$

can be written in the alternative form

$$v(k + 1) - \left(1 - \frac{1}{\tau}\right)v(k) = 0 \qquad (2.8)$$

simply by substituting $k + 1$ for k. You should convince yourself that the forms are equivalent. It is common when working with difference equations to rewrite them in terms of future or past time for mathematical convenience.

The characteristic equation for any difference equation can be formed by replacing each $v(k + n)$ term with the variable λ raised to the n power. The characteristic equation for Equation 2.8 is

$$\lambda^1 - \left(1 - \frac{1}{\tau}\right)\lambda^0 = 0 \tag{2.9}$$

or

$$\lambda - \left(1 - \frac{1}{\tau}\right) = 0$$

For difference equation Equation 2.5,

$$y(k + 2) - 3y(k + 1) + 2y(k) = 0$$

the characteristic equation is

$$\lambda^2 - 3\lambda + 2 = 0 \tag{2.10}$$

In general, for the difference is

$$a_n y(k + n) + a_{n-1} y(k + n - 1) + \cdots + a_1 y(k + 1) + a_0 y(k) = 0$$

the characteristic equation is the polynomial equation

$$a_n \lambda^n + a_{n-1} \lambda^{n-1} + \cdots + a_1 \lambda + a_0 = 0 \tag{2.11}$$

When the roots $\lambda_1, \ldots, \lambda_n$ of the characteristic equation are *distinct,* they provide an easy way of writing the closed-form solution of the difference equation. An nth-order difference equation will have an nth-order characteristic equation with n roots: $\lambda_1, \lambda_2, \ldots, \lambda_n$. As long as the roots are distinct, the solution to the difference equation is

$$y(k) = C_1 \lambda_1{}^k + C_2 \lambda_2{}^k + \cdots + C_n \lambda_n{}^k \tag{2.12}$$

where $C_1, C_2, \ldots, C_n$ are found from the initial conditions. Equation 2.9 has only one root, $\lambda = \left(1 - \frac{1}{\tau}\right)$, so the solution to the difference equation Equation 2.4 is

$$v(k) = C_1 \left(1 - \frac{1}{\tau}\right)^k \tag{2.13}$$

Since you know that $v(0) = v_0$, you can solve for C_1:

$$v(0) = C_1 \left(1 - \frac{1}{\tau}\right)^0 = v_0 \tag{2.14}$$

or

$$C_1 = v_0$$

The equation for the angular velocity as a function of time can be expressed as the closed-form equation

$$v(k) = v_0\left(1 - \frac{1}{\tau}\right)^k \tag{2.15}$$

You may recognize Equation 2.15 as the equation for exponential decay.

For the second-order difference equation, Equation 2.5, the roots of its characteristic equation (Equation 2.10) are $\lambda_1 = 1$ and $\lambda_2 = 2$, so the solution to the Equation 2.5 is

$$y(k) = C_1(1)^k + C_2(2)^k \tag{2.16}$$

Again, to solve for the values of C_1 and C_2, the value of $y(k)$ at two different time steps must be known. Using this information, you can write two equations with two unknowns, C_1 and C_2, which can be solved for C_1 and C_2.

Sequences of Solutions. Suppose that the random disturbances are now added to the equation for the angular velocity. The angular velocity at time k is the damped angular velocity at time $k - 1$ plus the random disturbances:

$$v(k) = \left(1 - \frac{1}{\tau}\right)v(k - 1) + r_{k-1} \tag{2.17}$$

or, in standard notation,

$$v(k) - \left(1 - \frac{1}{\tau}\right)v(k - 1) = r_{k-1} \tag{2.18}$$

where r_{k-1} is the random disturbance at time $k - 1$. Equation 2.18 is not a homogeneous equation because the right-hand side is no longer equal to zero. The right-hand side of a difference equation, $g(k)$, is called the *forcing* or *driving term*. For the case of the rocket, without the random disturbances, the angular velocity would decay to zero and the system would be in steady state; thus the random disturbances are said to drive the system.

Although methods exist in which nonhomogeneous equations can be solved using the characteristic function, another iterative approach is also possible. To solve Equation 2.18, you can start at $k = 1$, substituting $v(0)$ and r_0 into the equation and solving for $v(1)$; then move on to $k = 2$, substituting $v(1)$ and r_1 into the equation and solving for $v(2)$; and so on until $k = 6000$. This approach can be used in solving the rocket problem because r_k, the random disturbance at time k, can be read from the **file** at each time step. This approach will be completed at the end of the chapter in the solution to the case study.

Systems of Linear Difference Equations. In many applications, two or more equations may describe simultaneous, but different, aspects of an event. For the case study, the roll angle depends on the angular velocity, and both depend on time. The equation for the roll angle can be derived from the relationship between the distance traveled and the angular velocity as a function of time; that is, distance is velocity times time. Therefore, the distance, $\Delta d(k)$, traveled in time Δt is given by

$$\Delta d(k) = \Delta t\, v(k) \tag{2.19}$$

Because the time step, Δt, is 1 second, Δt can be dropped. So the position of the rocket at time k is the rocket's position at time $k - 1$ plus the change in position during time $k - 1$:

$$d(k) = d(k - 1) + v(k - 1) \tag{2.20}$$

where $d(k)$ is the roll angle at time k.

If random noise is ignored, the motion can be described by the equations

and
$$d(k) = d(k - 1) + v(k - 1)$$
$$v(k) = \left(1 - \frac{1}{\tau}\right)v(k - 1) \tag{2.21}$$

Equation 2.21 can be rewritten in matrix notation by making the following definitions:

$$y(k) = \begin{bmatrix} d(k) \\ v(k) \end{bmatrix} \qquad y(k - 1) = \begin{bmatrix} d(k - 1) \\ v(k - 1) \end{bmatrix}$$

$$A = \begin{bmatrix} 1 & 1 \\ 0 & \left(1 - \frac{1}{\tau}\right) \end{bmatrix}$$

In the definitions above, $y(k)$ is a vector of functions. In matrix form, the equations can be expressed as

$$y(k) = Ay(k - 1) \tag{2.22}$$

If you know the values of the coefficients for the initial conditions, $y(0)$, you can find a sequence of values for $y(k)$ for this system in the same way that a sequence of solutions was found for the single-equation system. Given the initial conditions, $y(1)$ can be found using matrix multiplication:

$$y(1) = Ay(0) \tag{2.23}$$

Once $y(1)$ is known, $y(2)$ can be found:

$$y(2) = Ay(1) \tag{2.24}$$

Substituting Equation 2.23 for $y(1)$ yields

$$y(2) = A^2 y(0) \tag{2.25}$$

And, in general,

$$y(k) = A^k y(0) \tag{2.26}$$

Could you rewrite the equations to include the random disturbances and still use the matrix-multiplication technique?

Solution to Case Study 2

Going back to the main program that was developed for the case study, you can see that the procedures that must be developed are **ComputeRollAngle, ReadRandom, ComputeAngularVelocity,** and **Report-ThisTime.** Two of the procedures are concerned with the discrete-time equations and two are concerned with files. The procedures concerned with discrete time systems will be developed first. The procedure **Compute-RollAngle** involves implementing Equation 2.20:

$$d(k) = d(k - 1) + v(k - 1)$$

Since $d(k - 1)$ and $v(k - 1)$ will be known, implementing this equation presents no problems. The original procedure heading included the variable **Step** for the time step,

```
ComputeRollAngle (Step, LastTime, ThisTime);
```

but the variable is not needed since Δt was assumed to equal one second, so **Step** can be eliminated from the procedure:

```
procedure ComputeRollAngle (Last : TimeRec;  var Current : TimeRec);
(*      Procedure ComputeRollAngle computes the current displacement,    *)
(*      Current.RollAngle, based on the values of the velocity and       *)
(*      roll angle from the previous time step.  Because the velocity    *)
(*      is in radians per second and the time step is one second, the    *)
(*      distance traveled in one second is the value of the velocity.    *)

begin
  Current.RollAngle := Last.RollAngle + Last.AngularVelocity
end; (* procedure ComputeRollAngle *)
```

Procedure **ComputeRollAngle** is a procedure that has only one executable statement. If the program is to be developed further so that the computation of the roll angle will be more complicated, **ComputeRollAngle** should be left as a procedure. If, on the other hand, no further refinements will be made, to avoid the overhead involved in creating and executing procedures, the procedure should be combined with another procedure.

Equation 2.18 can be used to compute the angular velocity. The procedure to compute the angular velocity is similar to procedure

ComputeRollAngle. Again the parameter **Step** can be eliminated, but a new parameter, the roll-time constant for the angular velocity decay, must be added.

```
procedure ComputeAngularVelocity (Noise, Tau : real;  Last : TimeRec;
                                   var Current : TimeRec);
(*      Procedure ComputeAngularVelocity computes the velocity at      *)
(*      the current time step based on the velocity at the previous    *)
(*      time step, the roll-time constant of the rocket and any random *)
(*      disturbances.                                                   *)

begin
   Current.AngularVelocity := (1.0 - 1.0/Tau) * Last.AngularVelocity + Noise
end; (* procedure ComputeAngularVelocity *)
```

The two procedures for reading from and writing to the **files** can be written easily because their data structures have been set up to match the information available at each time step in the program. In writing these procedures, the only decision that must be made is where the **files** are to be reset and rewritten. The **files** need only be reset/rewritten for the first time step. If the **files** are reset/rewritten within the procedures, a parameter for the time step must be passed and an **if** statement must be executed each time the procedure is executed to determine whether it is the first time step. It is more efficient to reset/rewrite the **files** at the beginning of the main program. The **file** procedures can be written as follows:

```
procedure ReadRandom (var Disturbance : real);
(*      Procedure ReadRandom reads the next entry in a file Random-  *)
(*      File which contains the values of the random disturbances.   *)

begin
   read (randomfile, Disturbance)
end; (* procedure ReadRandom *)
```

```
procedure ReportThisTime (Current : TimeRec);
(*      Procedure ReportThisTime writes the values stored in the   *)
(*      record for the current time step to the file, timefile.    *)

begin
   write (timefile, Current)
end; (* procedure ReportThisTime *)
```

Here is the final version of the program, incorporating all the changes
from the program development:

PROGRAM 2.1   RollingRocket

```
program RollingRocket (input, output, randomfile, timefile);
(*      Procedure RollingRocket simulates the data that will be        *)
(*      transmitted from a rocket.  The angular displacement and       *)
(*      angular velocity are computed every second for 6000 seconds.   *)
(*      The rocket is subject to random disturbances that change its   *)
(*      angular velocity.                                              *)

const MaxStep = 6000;                   (* maximum number of time steps. *)
      RollConstant = 10.65;             (* roll time decay constant. *)

type  TimeRec = record
         AngularVelocity : real;        (* angular velocity in radians/sec. *)
         RollAngle : real               (* angular displacement in radians. *)
      end; (* TimeRec *)

var   LastTime : TimeRec;               (* data for the last time step. *)
      ThisTime : TimeRec;               (* data for the current time step. *)
      Step : integer;                   (* counter for the time step number. *)
      Noise : real;                     (* random disturbance in the current *)
                                        (* time period. *)

      timefile : file of TimeRec;       (* output file of the data on each *)
                                        (* time step. *)

      randomfile : file of real;        (* input file of data for the random *)
                                        (* disturbance in each time period. *)

(*$i intitialize *)
(*$i computerollangle *)
(*$i readrandom *)
(*$i computeangularvelocity *)
(*$i reportthistime *)


(*----------------------------------------------------------------------*)

begin (* main *)
  reset (randomfile);
  rewrite (timefile);

  Initialize (Step, LastTime);

  repeat
    Step := Step + 1;
    ComputeRollAngle (LastTime, ThisTime);
```

```
   ReadRandom (Noise);
   ComputeAngularVelocity (Noise, RollConstant, LastTime, ThisTime);

   ReportThisTime (ThisTime);

   LastTime := ThisTime
 until Step > MaxStep;
 writeln(' The output is in the file time.fil.')
end. (* program RollingRocket *)
```

Problems

1. Which of the following equations are linear, homogeneous, constant coefficient difference equations? WHat is the order of each equation?

   (a) $(k + 1)y(k + 1) - ky(k) = 1$ (b) $y(k - 2) + 3y(k) - 5.5y(k + 2) = 0$

   (c) $y(k + 1) + 5y(k) - 3 = 0$ (d) $y(k + 1) = \dfrac{y(k)}{y(k + 2) - 23.6}$

2. Find a closed-form solution to each difference quation below. Use the resulting function to generate values of $y(k)$ for $k = 0, 1, 2, 3$, and 4, then graph $y(k)$ versus k.

   (a) $(k + 1) - \dfrac{1}{2}y(k) = 0,$ $y(0) = 1$

   (b) $y(k + 1) + \dfrac{1}{2}y(k) = 0,$ $y(0) = 1$

   (c) $2y(k + 2) - y(k + 1) - y(k) = 0,$ $y(0) = 2, y(1) = \dfrac{1}{2}$

   (d) $y(k + 2) - 2y(k + 1) + 2y(k) = 0,$ $y(0) = 2, y(1) = 2$

3. For Case Study 2, write the program that creates the file of 6000 real random numbers. The random disturbances are known to fall between -0.5 and 0.5 rad/s. Modify the function **RanNum** to return real numbers in the range -0.5 to 0.5.

4. A general, second-order, linear, homogeneous difference equation may be written as

$$y(k) = ay(k - 1) + by(k - 2)$$

   Write a program that requests values for a, b, $y(0)$, $y(1)$, and k and then recursively computes the value of $y(k)$.(See Chapter 15 in the main text.)

5. Five test rockets are fired at the same instant. Each rocket is identified by a ten-character code. The rocket's angular velocity, and its angular displacement

are computed each second. As soon as the angular velocity of any of the rockets exceeds 0.5 rad/sec, it explodes and the experiment stops, since all the other rockets are destroyed as well. The same equations that were used for Case Study 2 can be used to describe the angular displacement and angular velocity of each rocket. The time constant, τ, is equal to 10.0 for all the rockets. All the rockets are subject to the same noise.

Write a program that computes the angular velocity and displacement each second for each rocket until the experiment stops. Write the data for each rocket to a different file.

6. You are considering building a thermal-siphoning solar collector for a summer camp. In a thermal-siphoning solar collector, the storage tank is placed above the collector. No pumps are required to keep the water flowing: the water rises into the tank when the water is hot enough. When the sun does not shine, the water does not get hot, so the water does not circulate. You are trying to decide between two tanks: one is large and well insulated, the other is small and less well insulated. You want to know which one would have hotter water when the campers get up at sunrise. The sun always shines at the camp, so you are only worried about overnight storage. Assume that there are 14 hours of daylight, 10 hours of darkness each day, ans sunrise is at 6 a.m.

Using weather tapes supplied by the National Oceanic and Atmospheric Administration (NOAA), you have estimated the amount of energy you can collect in each hour on a sequence of three typical days in the summer. You also have collected data on the hourly hot water demand at the camp. This data has been stored in a computer file generated by the following program:

```
type  Energy = record
         SolarIn : real;     (* kiloJoules of energy from the collector into *)
                             (* the tank. *)
         Load : real         (* kiloJoules of hot water that leaves the tank. *)
      end;

var  KiloJ : array [1..24] of Energy;
     solarfile : file of Energy;

  rewrite (solarfile);
  for Day := 1 to 3 do
    for Hour := 1 to 24 do write (solarfile, KiloJ [Hour]);
```

The energy balance of the storage tank can be described by the difference equation below. The change in the temperature of the water in one hour is a function of the old temperature, the heat added from the collector, the heat that is lost as hot water is drawn from the tank, and heat lost through the walls of the tank.

$$T_{k+1} = T_k + \frac{\Delta t}{mC_p} [Q - L - (UA)(T_k - T_a)]$$

where T_k = temperature of the water at time k

  m = the mass of the water (kilograms)

  C_p = the specific heat of water (kilojoules per kilogram per °C)
         = 4.19 kJ/kg/°C

  Q = rate at which energy is added to the tank from the solar collector
         (kilojoules per hour)

  L = rate at which thermal energy is withdrawn from the tank
         (kilojoules per hour)

  UA = the loss coefficient of the tank times the surface area of the tank
         (kilojoules per hour per °C)

  Ta = the ambient temperature outside the tank (°C) = 20°C

  Δt = time increment = one hour

Q and L are the values that were stored in the Pascal file, solarfile.

Both tanks start out at 6 a.m. of the first day at 45°C. The first storage tank can hold 1500 kg of water, and its loss coefficient, UA, is 40. The second storage tank can hold 1000 kg of water, and its loss coefficient is 60. Print the temperature at 6 p.m., midnight, and 6 a.m. for each day for each tank. Have the program print out which tank produces hotter water on the average.

APPLICATION 3
Numerical Differentiation

CASE STUDY 3
The path of a particle

Suppose that a particle is constrained to move along a curve described by the function

$$y = x^5 - 2x^4 + x^3 \tag{3.1}$$

Equation 3.1 is plotted in Figure 3.1

At the points marked a, b, and c, the particle is momentarily at rest because the change in the y direction for a small change in the x direction is 0. At point a, the particle is at a relative maximum because the curve rises to point a and then decreases. At point c, the particle is at a relative minimum because the curve decreases to the point and then rises. At point b (a point of inflection), the particle is not at a maximum or a minimum because the direction of the curve does not change as it passes through the point. The conditions for a particle being at rest and being at a maximum or a minimum are:

if $f'(x) = 0$	the particle is at rest
if $f'(x) = 0$ and $f''(x) > 0$	the particle is at a minimum
if $f'(x) = 0$ and $f''(x) < 0$	the particle is at a maximum
if $f'(x) = 0$ and $f''(x) = 0$	the test fails

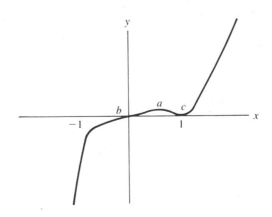

FIGURE 3.1
The path of a particle.

where $f'(x)$ is the first derivative of the function and $f''(x)$ is the second derivative of the function.

Write Pascal functions that compute the first and second derivatives of a function in the form $y = f(x)$. Use these functions in a program that computes the first and second derivatives for the particle as it moves along the path from $x = -1.0$ to $x = 2.0$. Print a table of the position, first derivative, and second derivative at intervals of length 0.5 From this table, deduce the points at which the particle is at rest, at a maximum, and at a minimum.

Algorithm development

The problem for the case study can be restated as follows: Given the equation $y = f(x)$ of the path of motion of the particle, compute y, $f'(x)$, and $f''(x)$ for values of x ranging from -1.0 to 2.0 at intervals of length 0.5, and report the values in a table. Knowing that the algorithms for computing the first and second derivative will be developed in this section, Algorithm 3.1 is the first iteration for the solution to the case study.

ALGORITHM 3.1   Algorithm for finding minima and maxima of a particle

begin algorithm

   1. Initialize the program
      a. Read the parameters that describe the particle
         read **FirstX,** the value of x where the particle starts
         read **LastX,** the value of x where the particle finishes
         read **XIncrement,** the length of the increment along the
         x-axis for which values should be computed
      b. **X ← FirstX**
   2. Compute the values of **Y,** $f'(\mathbf{X})$, and $f''(\mathbf{x})$
      while **X <= LastX** do
        begin
          Y ← $f(\mathbf{X})$
          YPrime ← $f'(\mathbf{X})$
          YDoublePrime ← $f''(\mathbf{x})$
          X ← X + XIncrement
          Report **Y, YPrime,** and **YDoublePrime**
        end while
  end algorithm

In writing Algorithm 3.1 several decisions were made. The decision to report the values of y, $f'(x)$, and $f''(x)$ as soon as they are computed, rather than saving them in arrays, has the greatest effect on the final program. This decision requires that the reporting procedure be included within the **while-do** loop. A **while-do** loop instead of a **for** loop was chosen to allow the user flexibility in choosing the increment for the x-coordinate.

Numerical differentiation

Computing the maxima and minima of Equation 3.1 in a Pascal program will require taking the derivative of the function $f(x)$. The first derivative $f'(x)$ gives the slope of a line drawn tangent to the curve at a particular value of x. This is equivalent to the change in y for a small change in x divided by the small change in x. If the slope of the tangent line is positive, the curve described by $f(x)$ will be rising at that point. If the slope is negative, the curve will be descending. If the slope is zero, the tangent line is parallel to the x-axis, the curve is neither rising nor descending, and the point may be a minimum point, a maximum point, or a point of inflection.

The second derivative $f''(x)$ is the derivative of the first derivative and thus describes the slope of a line drawn tangent to the curve of the first derivative at the point x. The second derivative can be used to test whether a function is concave up or concave down at a point x. If $f''(x) < 0$, the curve is concave down (it spills water) and the point x is a relative maximum. If $f''(x) > 0$, the curve is concave up (it holds water) and the point x is a relative minimum. These two conditions are illustrated in Figure 3.2. If $f''(x)$ equals 0, the second derivative test fails.

Sometimes it is possible, and desirable, to evaluate $f'(x)$ and $f''(x)$ using differential calculus. For example, if you were working with the equation $f(x) = 2x^3$, a knowledge of calculus would allow you to immediately write $f'(x) = 6x^2$. Within a program, however, there is no general algorithm that will allow you to find the functional form of $f'(x)$. Therefore, it is necessary to write a function that uses numerical methods to find an approximate value for the derivative of $f(x)$ for a particular value of x.

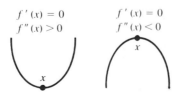

$f'(x) = 0$
$f''(x) > 0$

$f'(x) = 0$
$f''(x) < 0$

x

x

FIGURE 3.2
Relative minimum and maximum.

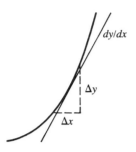

FIGURE 3.3
The slope dy/dx and the slope $\Delta y/\Delta x$.

The first derivative

The derivative of $f(x)$ can be found by taking the limit as the change in x, Δx, approaches 0:

$$\frac{dy}{dx} = \lim_{\Delta x \to 0} \frac{f(x + \Delta x) - f(x)}{\Delta x} \tag{3.2}$$

Equation 3.2 suggests that one method for computing the derivative on a computer would be to evaluate the right-hand side using a small value of Δx:

$$\frac{dy}{dx} \cong \frac{\Delta y}{\Delta x} = \frac{f(x + \Delta x) - f(x)}{\Delta x} \tag{3.3}$$

Figure 3.3 illustrates two lines: one with the slope of the derivative and the other with the slope $\Delta y/\Delta x$. This figure shows that Equation 3.3 gives a one-sided approximation for the derivative.

A more accurate approximation for the slope of the curve at point x would be the average of two slopes, one taken at $x + \Delta x$ and the other taken at $x - \Delta x$, as illustrated in Figure 3.4.

Mathematically, the approximation for the derivative illustrated in Figure 3.4 is

$$\frac{\Delta y}{\Delta x} = \frac{1}{2}\left[\frac{f(x + \Delta x) - f(x)}{\Delta x} + \frac{f(x - \Delta x) - f(x)}{-\Delta x}\right] \tag{3.4}$$

or

$$f'(x) \cong \frac{\Delta y}{\Delta x} = \frac{f(x + \Delta x) - f(x - \Delta x)}{2\Delta x} \tag{3.5}$$

If a Pascal function **Curve** has been defined, the approximation for the derivative can be evaluated using the statement

```
Derivative := (Curve(X + DeltaX) - Curve(X - DeltaX)) / (2 * DeltaX)
```

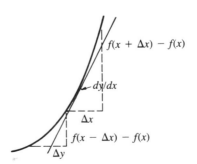

FIGURE 3.4
Approximating the derivative with the average of two lines.

How small should **DeltaX** be? Based on the definition of the derivative from Equation 3.2, you may think it should be as small as possible. But, because of the numerical errors inherent in computer calculations, if **DeltaX** is made as small as possible, there will be almost no difference between the function evaluated at **X + DeltaX** and the function evaluated at **X − DeltaX**. The number of significant digits stored by the computer will not be sufficient to accurately express the difference between the two values. When the small and inaccurate number representing Δy is then divided by 2 times the small number **DeltaX,** the result will be a poor approximation of the derivative. You must choose a value of **DeltaX** that is small enough that the assumptions used in computing the numerical derivative are not violated, but large enough that the answer is not lost in the rounding error of the computer. The choice of a good value will depend on the number of significant digits that your computer stores.

The function **Derivative** takes the derivative of any mathematical function of the form $y = f(x)$. In this function, **DeltaX** is specified as a local constant instead of being declared in the parameter list. This is a precaution to prevent an unwary user from specifying a **DeltaX** that is too small.

```
function Derivative (function Curve (Z : real) : real; X : real) : real;
(*      This function returns the derivative of the function passed as      *)
(*      Curve evaluated at the point X using a two-sided derivative.        *)

const DeltaX = 5.0e-2;        (* DeltaX must not be too small or the deriva- *)
                             (* tive will be lost in the rounding error, but *)
                             (* if DeltaX is too large the approximation for *)
                             (* the derivative will be poor. *)

begin
  Derivative := (Curve(X + DeltaX) - Curve(X - DeltaX)) / (2 * DeltaX)
end; (* function Derivative *)
```

The second derivative

The second derivative of a function is the change in the first derivative of the function with respect to a change in x; that is, it is the derivative of the first derivative. The second derivative is written as

$$f''(x) = \frac{d^2y}{dx^2} = \frac{d}{dx}\frac{dy}{dx}$$

or   (3.6)

$$f''(x) = \frac{d}{dx}f'(x)$$

Substituting $f'(x)$ for $f(x)$ in Equation 3.5, which was used to compute the first derivative, results in Equation 3.7, which can be used to approximate the second derivative.

$$f''(x) \cong \frac{f'(x + \Delta x) - f'(x - \Delta x)}{2\Delta x} \tag{3.7}$$

The first derivatives in Equation 3.7 can be approximated by substituting Equation 3.4 evaluated at $f'(x + \Delta x)$ and $f'(x - \Delta x)$ for the first derivatives:

$$f''(x) \cong \frac{1}{2\Delta x}\left[\frac{f(x + 2\Delta x) - f(x)}{2\Delta x} - \frac{f(x - 2\Delta x) - f(x)}{-2\Delta x}\right]$$

$$\cong \frac{f(x + 2\Delta x) - 2f(x) + f(x - 2\Delta x)}{(2\Delta x)^2} \tag{3.8}$$

Equation 3.8 can be simplified by replacing $2\Delta x$ by Δx, as shown in Equation 3.9.

$$f''(x) \cong \frac{f(x + \Delta x) - 2f(x) + f(x - \Delta x)}{\Delta x^2} \tag{3.9}$$

Equation 3.9 evaluates the second derivative without evaluating the first derivative. The following Pascal function uses this equation to return the **SecondDerivative** of a function:

```
function SecondDerivative (function Curve(Z : real) : real; X : real) : real;
(*      This function returns the second derivative of the function       *)
(*      passed as Curve evaluated at the point X using a two-sided        *)
(*      derivative.                                                       *)

const DeltaX = 5.0e-2;        (* DeltaX must not be too small or the deriva- *)
                              (* tive will be lost in the rounding error, but *)
                              (* if DeltaX is too large the approximation for *)
                              (* the derivative will be poor. *)

begin
  SecondDerivative := (Curve(X + DeltaX) - 2 * Curve(X) + Curve(X - DeltaX))
                   / sqr (DeltaX)
end; (* function SecondDerivative *)
```

Problems with numerical approximations of derivatives

Taking derivatives numerically has several pitfalls. Any numerical derivative is subject to errors due to rounding and truncation, as previously discussed. Other unrelated problems occur when a function is changing

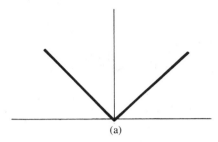
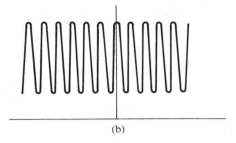

(a)   (b)

FIGURE 3.5
Conditions for which numerical differentiation is invalid.

rapidly or is undifferentiable at a point. Both conditions are illustrated in Figure 3.5.

The function abs(x) in Figure 3.5(a) is not differentiable at the point 0, that is, the derivative is undefined at 0. Mathematically, the problem arises because the slope of the function is positive if the point 0 is approached from right and negative if approached from the left. But if the function **Derivative** is executed for the function abs(0), it will return a value for the derivative. There is no indication that the value returned by the function is nonsense; therefore, whenever you perform numerical differentiation within a program, you must be sure that the function is differentiable. Mathematical tests for differentiability are beyond the scope of this text, but can be found in introductory calculus books.

The function $f(x)$ in Figure 3.5(b) changes rapidly over a distance on the order of Δx. If the size of **DeltaX** in the program is reduced, truncation errors will occur. Curves that behave like the one in Figure 3.5(b) can be identified mathematically by the fact that $f''(x)$ is large. But for the same reasons that $f'(x)$ cannot be computed numerically if Δx is small, $f''(x)$ cannot be computed numerically, so the test cannot be performed with confidence within the program. Before performing numerical differentiation, you must be sure the curve is not changing rapidly in the area where the derivatives are being computed.

Solution to Case Study 3

Algorithm 3.1 can be translated into a Pascal program using the functions **Derivative** and **SecondDerivative.** Most of the additional procedures in the program are required for input/output.

PROGRAM 3.1   Particle

```
program Particle (input, output);
(*      This program follows the path of a particle along a curve and      *)
(*      computes the first and second derivatives at specified intervals.  *)

var    FirstX : real;           (* point on X-axis where particle starts. *)
       LastX : real;            (* point on X-axis where particle stops. *)
       IncrementX : real;       (* increment at which position is computed. *)


(*$i ztopower *)
(*$i derivative *)
(*$i secondderivative *)


  function Path (X : real) : real;
  (*      Path returns the Y displacement of the particle given the X      *)
  (*      displacement.                                                    *)

  begin
    Path := ZToPower(X, 5) - (2 * ZToPower(X, 4)) + ZToPower(X, 3)
  end; (* function Path *)


(*$i firstmessage *)
(*  procedure FirstMessage;                                                *)
(*      This procedure writes the initial message to the program user.    *)


(*$i readdata *)
(*  procedure ReadData (var XFirst, XLast, XIncrement : real);            *)
(*      ReadData reads the initial and final displacement of the          *)
(*      particle from the terminal and reads the increment at which       *)
(*      the points are to be computed.  It also writes the headings       *)
(*      for the output tables.                                            *)


(*$i report *)
(*  procedure Report (XValue, YValue, FirstD, SecondD : real);           *)
(*      This procedure prints the current values for X, Y, and the        *)
(*      first and second derivatives.                                     *)
```

```
procedure ComputeAndReportDerivatives (XFirst, XLast, XIncrement : real);
(*      Procedure Report that reports the values of the derivatives.    *)

var   X : real;               (* current X position of the particle. *)
      Y : real;               (* current Y position of the particle. *)
      YPrime : real;          (* first derivative of function. *)
      YDoublePrime : real;    (* second derivative of function. *)

begin
  X := XFirst;
  while X <= XLast do
    begin
      Y := Path(X);
      YPrime := Derivative (Path, X);
      YDoublePrime := SecondDerivative (Path, X);

      Report (X, Y, YPrime, YDoublePrime);
      X := X + XIncrement
    end (* while *)
end; (* procedure ComputeAndReportDerivatives *)


(*----------------------------------------------------------------------*)
begin (* main program *)
  FirstMessage;

  ReadData (FirstX, LastX, IncrementX);

  ComputeAndReportDerivatives (FirstX, LastX, IncrementX)
end. (* program Particle *)
```

=>
 This program follows a particle along a path
 and reports its X and Y displacements.

 The program also reports the first and second derivatives.
 The particle is at a minimum when the first derivative
 equals zero and the second derivative is greater than zero.

 The particle is at a maximum when the first derivative
 equals zero and the second derivative is less than zero.

 What is the initial displacement of the particle?
 □-1.0
 What is the final displacement of the particle?
 □2.0
 What is the incremental value of X?
 □0.25

X	Y	First Derivative	Second Derivative
-1.0000	-4.0000	16.0475	-50.0350
-0.7500	-1.2920	6.6761	-26.4662
-0.5000	-0.2813	2.0813	-11.5225
-0.2500	-0.0244	0.3411	-3.3287
0.0000	0.0000	0.0025	-0.0100
0.2500	0.0088	0.0811	0.3087
0.5000	0.0313	0.0613	-0.4975
0.7500	0.0264	-0.1039	-0.5537
1.0000	0.0000	0.0075	2.0150
1.2500	0.1221	1.2861	9.0837
1.5000	0.8438	5.0913	22.5275
1.7500	3.0146	13.2511	44.2212
2.0000	8.0000	28.0625	76.0400

The minima and maxima of the function $y = x^5 - 2x^4 + x^3$ can be found from the output table of values. In the table, $f'(x)$ is identically equal to 0 at $x = 0.0$, $y = 0.0$ and at $x = 1.0$, $y = 0.0$. At the point (0.0, 0.0), the second derivative is also 0, so the second derivative fails. (The particle is at a point of inflection.) At the point (1.0, 0.0), the second derivative is positive, so the particle is at a minimum at (1.0, 0.0). Even though the value $f'(x)$ is not equal to 0 at any other tabulated point, the sign of $f'(x)$ changes between $x = 0.50$ and $x = 0.75$. Therefore, $f'(x)$ must be equal to 0 at some point between these points. Because the second derivative for these values is negative, the particle is at a maximum somewhere between the points (0.50, 0.031) and (0.75, 0.026). In the application, *Finding Roots of Equations*, a technique will be developed that will allow you to determine the exact value of x for which $f'(x)$ is equal to 0.

Problems

1. Expand Program 3.1, **Particle,** to plot the path of the particle.

2. Given that the derivative of cos x is $-\sin x$, that is,

$$\frac{d \cos x}{dx} = -\sin x$$

write a program to test the accuracy of **Derivative.** Compute the derivative over a range of values Δx using numerical differentiation. The program should write a table that reports the relative error for the values of Δx. Assume the value returned by the standard function **sin** is the true value.

3. Find the minimum or maximum point of the function

$$y = ax^2 + bx + c$$

using the functions **Derivative** and **SecondDerivative.** Test your program with $a = 9.0$, $b = 3.5$, and $c = 1.2$. Test it again with $a = -9.0$, $b = 3.5$, and $c = 1.2$.

APPLICATION 4
Numerical Integration

CASE STUDY 4
Tabulating the Gaussian distribution

The Gaussian, or normal, distribution covered in the application section of Chapter 10 in the main text is often used in the statistical analysis of experiments. A random variable that has a Gaussian distribution with a mean of 0.0 and a variance of 1.0 is referred to as a *standardized normal random variable*. The formula for the probability density function of a standardized normal random variable x is given in Equation 4.1 and is illustrated in Figure 4.1.

$$f(x) = \frac{1}{(2\pi)^{-1/2}} e^{-x^2/2} \tag{4.1}$$

The probability that a standardized normal variable X takes on a value between a and b is the integral of the function $f(x)$ between a and b:

$$P(a<X<b) = \int_a^b f(x)\ dx \tag{4.2}$$

Equation 4.2 cannot be solved in a closed form. In other words, the probability that X lies between a and b cannot be found by using standard integration techniques. Instead, numerical techniques are used to create tables so that $P(a < X < b)$ can be evaluated.

Write a program that prints a table of $P(a < X < x)$ for twenty values of x between the fixed value of a and an upper bound b. As part of the program, write a general function that computes the integral between two values on any curve in the form $y = f(x)$.

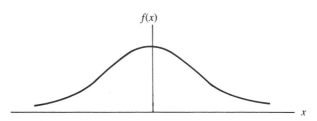

FIGURE 4.1
The density function of a standardized normal random variable.

Algorithm development

Using the top-down design approach, assume that an algorithm for computing the integral can be developed. In Step 2 of Algorithm 4.1, the Pascal function **Integral(Normal, FirstX, CurrentX)** will return the integral of the mathematical function **Normal** between **FirstX** and **CurrentX**.

ALGORITHM 4.1   Algorithm to compute a table for $P(a < X < x)$

begin algorithm
1. Initialize the program
   a. Read **FirstX** and **LastX**
   b. **CurrentX** ← **FirstX**
   c. **Increment** ← (**LastX** − **FirstX**) / 20
2. Compute P(**FirstX** < **X** < **CurrentX**) for **CurrentX** from **FirstX** to **LastX**
   while **CurrentX** <= **LastX** do
     begin
         Y ← **Integral(Normal, FirstX, CurrentX)**
         Save **CurrentX** and **Y**
         CurrentX ← **CurrentX** + **Increment**
     end
3. Print a table of values for all **CurrentX** and **Y**
end algorithm

Numerical integration

One interpretation of the integral of a function is that it is the area under the curve between the upper and lower limits. For example, in Figure 4.2 the

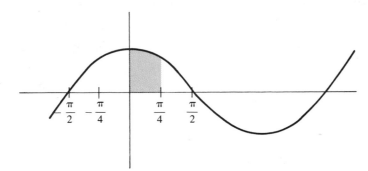

FIGURE 4.2
The integral of cos x from 0 to $\pi/4$.

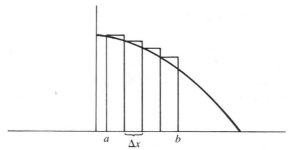

FIGURE 4.3
Using rectangles to approximate
the area under a curve.

integral of the cosine function between 0 and $\pi/4$ is the shaded area. For many functions, the integral can be expressed as another function. For example, the integral of the cosine is the sine. It is, however, difficult to program a digital computer to evaluate the integral and produce a generalized function. Instead, computers are programmed to perform *numerical integration* in which the numerical value of the integral is computed for particular values of the limits a and b.

In numerical integration, the area under a function is approximated by the sum of the areas of geometric forms. The basic idea is to create forms that approximate the curve at each point, as illustrated in Figure 4.3, in which rectangles are used to approximate the area.

As Figure 4.3 shows, rectangles do not always give a good approximation to the area. A more accurate approach to approximating the area under a curve $f(x)$ between points a and b is to use trapezoids. The area A of each trapezoid i is

$$A_i = \Delta x \frac{f(x_{i-1}) + f(x_i)}{2} \tag{4.3}$$

where $f(x_i)$ = the function evaluated at the point x_i

Δx = the length of the interval on the x-axis = $x_i - x_{i-1}$

The areas described by Equation 4.3 are illustrated in Figure 4.4.

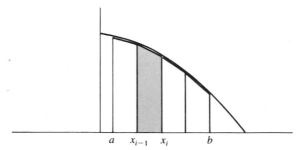

FIGURE 4.4
The area between a and b
approximated by trapezoids.

If the x-axis is divided into n equal intervals of length Δx and the area above each interval is approximated by a trapezoid, the total area under the curve A is

$$A = \Delta x \sum_{i=1}^{n-1} \frac{f(x_i) + f(x_{i+1})}{2} \qquad (4.4)$$

Equation 4.4 can be simplified to

$$A = \Delta x \frac{f(x_1) + f(x_n)}{2} + \sum_{i=2}^{n-1} f(x_i) \qquad (4.5)$$

Equation 4.5 is called the *trapezoidal rule.*

The trapezoidal rule can be implemented as a Pascal function using a **for** statement. The Pascal function will be able to compute the area under any curve $f(x)$ if the curve is passed in the parameter list. The function **Trapezoid** computes the area under the Pascal function **Curve,** given the number of intervals and the initial and final values of x.

```
function Trapezoid (function Curve (Z : real) : real; XFirst, XLast : real;
               NumIntervals : integer) : real;
(*      This function returns the area under the curve Curve(X) between     *)
(*      XFirst and XLast by approximating the area with trapezoids and      *)
(*      using Equation 15.21.  The X-axis is divided into NumIntervals.     *)

var    Area : real;        (* intermediate variable for the function value. *)
       Index : integer;    (* for statement control variable. *)
       DeltaX : real;      (* length of each segment on the X-axis. *)
       X : real;           (* value of X within the for statement. *)

begin
   DeltaX := (XLast - XFirst) / NumIntervals;   (* compute the length of *)
                                                (* interval on the X-axis. *)
   Area := (Curve(XFirst) + Curve(XLast)) / 2.0;  (* initialize Area to 1/2 *)
                                                (* the sum of the values *)
                                                (* at the end points. *)

   for Index := 1 to NumIntervals - 1 do
     begin
       X := XFirst + Index * DeltaX;            (* compute X for the *)
                                                (* current index. *)

       Area := Area + Curve(X)                  (* add the value of the *)
                                                (* function at X to Area. *)
     end; (* for *)
   Trapezoid := Area * DeltaX
end; (* function Trapezoid *)
```

A refinement of the trapezoidal rule is *Simpson's method* for computing the area under a curve. Simpson's method replaces the straight line at the top of the trapezoids with the arc of a parabola, giving an even better approximation of the curve. This geometric form is illustrated in Figure 4.5.

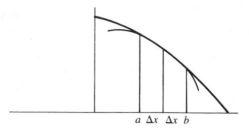

FIGURE 4.5
The area under a curve
approximated by a parabolic arc.

The area under the curve between the points $x - \Delta x$ and $x + \Delta x$ can be determined by using the equation for a parabolic arc, as follows:

$$A_i = \frac{\Delta x}{3} \left[f(x - \Delta x) + 4f(x) + f(x + \Delta x) \right] \qquad (4.6)$$

Given that the interval pictured in Figure 4.5 is $2\Delta x$, and that the area calculated in Equation 4.6 is the area under the curve for the interval $2\Delta x$, the total area under the curve $f(x)$ is

$$A = \frac{\Delta x}{3} \left[f(x_0) + 4f(x_1) + f(x_2) \right] + \left[f(x_2) + 4f(x_3) + f(x_4) \right]$$

$$+ \cdots + \left[f(x_{n-2}) + 4f(x_{n-1}) + f(x_n) \right] \qquad (4.7)$$

or

$$A = \frac{\Delta x}{3} \left[f(x_0) + 4f(x_1) + 2f(x_2) + 4f(x_3) \right.$$

$$+ \cdots + 2f(x_{n-2}) + 4f(x_{n-1}) + f(x_n) \right] \qquad (4.8)$$

The Pascal function **Simpson** computes the area under a curve given the function, the number of intervals, and the initial and final values of x:

```
function Simpson (Curve (Z : real) : real; XFirst, XLast : real;
              NumIntervals : integer) : real;
   (*     This function returns the area under the curve Curve(X) between    *)
   (*     XFirst and XLast by approximating the area with arcs of para-      *)
   (*     bolas using Simpson's rule (Equation 15.24).  The X-axis is        *)
   (*     is divided into NumIntervals which must be an even number.         *)

   var   Area : real;        (* intermediate variable for the function value. *)
         Index : integer;    (* for statement control variable. *)
         DeltaX : real;      (* length of each segment on the X-axis. *)
         X : real;           (* value of X within the for statement. *)
```

```
begin
  if odd (NumIntervals) then                    (* force NumIntervals to *)
    NumIntervals := NumIntervals + 1;           (* be even. *)

  Area := 0.0;                                  (* initialize Area. *)
  DeltaX := (XLast - XFirst) / NumIntervals;    (* compute the length of *)
                                                (* interval on the X-axis. *)

  for Index := 1 to NumIntervals - 1 do
    begin
      X := XFirst + Index * DeltaX;
      if odd (Index) then                       (* if Index is odd, *)
        Area := Area + 4 * Curve(X)             (* multiply F(X) by 4. *)
      else                                      (* if Index is even, *)
        Area := Area + 2 * Curve(X)            (* multiply F(X) by 2. *)
    end; (* for *)

  Simpson := DeltaX * (Area + Curve (XFirst) + Curve (XLast)) / 3.0
end; (* function Simpson *)
```

The only restriction on the use of this method is that the number of intervals n must be an even number so that there are three points for every parabola.

Solution to Case Study 4

Algorithm 4.1 can be translated into the Pascal program **NormalTable,** using the function **Simpson.**

PROGRAM 4.1 NormalTable

```
program NormalTable (input, output);
(*      This program prints a table of the probability that a standard-    *)
(*      ized normal random variable lies between a and b for a range of    *)
(*      b.  It uses Simpson's rule to integrate the area under the curve.  *)

const NumEntries = 20;        (* number of entries in the output table. *)
      NumIntervals = 20;      (* number of intervals used in computation of *)
                              (* the area. *)

var   FirstZ : real;          (* lower value of Z. *)
      LastZ : real;           (* upper value of Z. *)


(*$i printmessage *)
(*  procedure PrintMessage;                                                *)
(*      Procedure PrintMessage prints a message to the program user.       *)
```

```
(*$i readz *)
(*   procedure Readz (var ZFirst, ZLast : real);                          *)
(*        This procedure reads the first value of Z and the last value    *)
(*        of Z from the user at the terminal.                             *)


(*$i tablehead *)
(*   procedure TableHead (ZFirst : real);                                 *)
(*        This procedure writes the heading for the table of values of    *)
(*        the normal distribution.                                        *)


  function ProbDensity (Z : real) : real;
  (*      Function ProbDensity returns the value of f(z), the probab-     *)
  (*      ility density function of the normal distribution.              *)

  const Pi = 3.14159;

  begin
    ProbDensity := exp (-sqr(Z) / 2.0) / sqrt(2.0 * Pi)
  end; (* function ProbDensity *)


(*$i simpson *)

  procedure ComputeAndPrintTable (ZFirst, ZLast : real)
  (*      This procedure computes the P (ZFirst < Z < ZLast) over the     *)
  (*      range of values for ZLast.  It uses the function Simpson to     *)
  (*      compute the area under the curve stored in ProbDensity.  It     *)
  (*      references the two global constants NumEntries, the number of   *)
  (*      entries in the table, and NumIntervals, which is the number of  *)
  (*      intervals to be used in computing the area.                     *)

  var   Num : integer;          (* for statement control variable. *)
        Probability : real;     (* local variable to store probability. *)
        Inc : real;             (* increment of entries in the table. *)
        Z : real;               (* current value of the upper bound. *)

  begin
    Inc := (ZLast - ZFirst) / NumEntries;
    for Num := 0 to NumEntries do
      begin
        Z := ZFirst + Inc * Num;
        Probability := Simpson (ProbDensity, ZFirst, Z, NumIntervals);
        writeln (Z:11:2, Probability:15:5)
      end (* for *)
  end; (* procedure ComputeAndPrintTable *)
```

```
(*-----------------------------------------------------------------*)
begin (* main program *)
  PrintMessage;
  ReadZ (FirstZ, LastZ);
  TableHead (FirstZ);
  ComputeAndPrintTable (FirstZ, LastZ):
end. (* program NormalTable *)

=>
 This program prints a table of the probability that a normal
 random variable is greater than a and less than z for
 20 values of z between a and b.

 Enter a value for a, the lower value
 □-4.0
 Enter a value for b, the upper value
 □4.0

 For a standardized normal random variable, Z,
 with a mean of 0.0 and a variance of 1.0

         z         P( -4.0 < Z < z)

      -4.00          0.00000
      -3.60          0.00013
      -3.20          0.00066
      -2.80          0.00252
      -2.40          0.00817
      -2.00          0.02272
      -1.60          0.05477
      -1.20          0.11504
      -0.80          0.21182
      -0.40          0.34454
      -0.00          0.49997
       0.40          0.65540
       0.80          0.78812
       1.20          0.88491
       1.60          0.94517
       2.00          0.97721
       2.40          0.99176
       2.80          0.99741
       3.20          0.99928
       3.60          0.99981
       4.00          0.99994
```

You can test the difference in accuracy between the functions **Simpson** and **Trapezoid** by computing the values of $P(-\infty < X < x)$ with both functions and then comparing your computed values to the values in Table 4.1. Because you cannot start the interval at minus infinity, you may be tempted to start it at a number such as $-1.0e30$. The strategy will, however, increase the computation time and will not increase the accuracy of the computation because Δx will be too large. A better strategy would be to set the lower bound to a number such as -5.0, since almost 100 percent of the area is within ± 4 standard deviations of the mean in a Gaussian distribution, as you can see from Table 4.1.

TABLE 4.1
Tabulation of the Gaussian distribution

$$\Phi(z) = \int_{-\infty}^{z} \frac{1}{(2\pi)^{1/2}} e^{-x^2/2} \, dx = P(Z < z)$$

z	$\Phi(z)$	z	$\Phi(z)$	z	$\Phi(z)$	z	$\Phi(z)$
0.0	0.5000	1.0	0.8413	2.0	0.9772	3.0	0.9986
0.1	0.5398	1.1	0.8643	2.1	0.9821	3.1	0.9990
0.2	0.5793	1.2	0.8849	2.2	0.9861	3.2	0.9993
0.3	0.6179	1.3	0.9032	2.3	0.9893	3.3	0.9995
0.4	0.6554	1.4	0.9192	2.4	0.9918	3.4	0.9997
0.5	0.6915	1.5	0.9332	2.5	0.9938	3.5	0.99977
0.6	0.7257	1.6	0.9452	2.6	0.9953	3.6	0.99984
0.7	0.7580	1.7	0.9554	2.7	0.9965	3.7	0.99989
0.8	0.7881	1.8	0.9641	2.8	0.9974	3.8	0.99993
0.9	0.8159	1.9	0.9713	2.9	0.9981	3.9	0.99995

Problems

1. To analyze a reaction involving carbon dioxide, Co_2, the absolute entropy S_T of CO_2 at a temperature T K and 1.0 atm must be calculated. The relationship between the absolute entropy and the temperature is given by

$$S_T = S_{T0} + \int_{T0}^{T} \frac{C_p}{T_0} \, dT$$

where T_0 = 298.1 K

S_T = absolute entropy of CO_2 at T degrees Kelvin

S_{T0} = absolute entropy of CO_2 at 298.1 K

  = 213.7 J K^{-1} mole^{-1}

C_p = the heat capacity at constant pressure in joules per Kelvin-mole

The following table gives values of C_p for CO_2 over a range of temperatures.

Temperature (K)	Heat Capacity (J-mole)
298.1	37.15
300.0	37.29
400.0	42.36
500.0	45.18
600.0	47.11
700.0	48.62
800.0	49.92
900.0	51.08
1000.0	52.16

Write a program that returns the absolute entropy for CO_2 at 1 atm of pressure for any temperature between T_0 and 1000 K.

2. Given that the integral of the sine is the cosine, that is

$$\int_a^b \cos x \, dx = \sin b - \sin a$$

write a program to compare the accuracy of **Trapezoid** and **Simpson** over a range of values of a and b. Report the relative error for each method with respect to the value computed using the standard function **sin.**

3. In a microphone, a membrane is driven by a sinusoidal pressure to convert sound into a voltage. The wave pattern produced in the membrane can be described by a differential equation. Solving the differential equation results in the following equation for the amplitude ψ of the displacement at a point that is a distance a from the edge of the membrane:

$$\psi = \frac{P}{(2\pi f/c)^2 T} \frac{J_0(2\pi fr/c)}{[J_0(2\pi fa/c)]} - 1.0$$

where P = the amplitude of the driving pressure in pascals

T = the tension on the membrane in newtons

a = the radial distance from the edge in meters

r = the radius of the membrane in meters

f = the frequence in hertz

c = the speed of sound in the membrane in meters per second

and $J_0(x)$ is the Bessel function of order 0:

$$J_0(x) = \sum_{i=1}^{\infty} \frac{(-1)^k \left(\frac{x}{2}\right)^{2k}}{(k!)^2}$$

Write a function that returns the sum of the first ten terms of the Bessel function of order zero. Using this function, write another function that returns the amplitude of displacement for a microphone, given the distance a from the edge and the frequency f. In the case under study, the microphone has a radius of 0.15 m, the amplitude of the pressure is 6000 pa, and the tension is 10,000 N/m. Under these conditions, the speed of sound in the membrane is 81.65 m/s.

Write a program that computes the amplitude of the displacement for the membrane when it is driven at a frequency of 400 Hz. Compute the amplitude at the edge ($a = 0$), at a distance of one-quarter the radius, at a distance of one-half the radius, and at the center ($a = r$).

4. The Bessel function of order 0 given in Problem 3 can also be written in the integral form

$$J_0(x) = \frac{2}{\pi} \int_0^{\pi/2} \cos(x \sin t) \, dt$$

Write a function that uses numerical integration to evaluate the Bessel function. Write another function that evaluates the Bessel function using the first ten terms of the series equation from Problem 3. Write a program that invokes both functions for $x = 1, 2, \ldots, 10$ and compares the results.

5. Another method of computing the integral of a curve, using random number generators, is called *Monte Carlo* integration. Monte Carlo integration works on the following analogy: If you throw darts at a dart board in a completely random fashion, you would expect the fraction of tosses that land in a particular sector to be equal to that sector's proportion of the total area. For example, if you randomly hit a dart board with 1000 darts and 100 of the darts land in one sector, you can conclude that the sector is one-tenth the area of the dart board. To apply the same principle to computing the area under a curve, draw a rectangle that has a base of length ($b - a$) and a height of max [$f(a)$, $f(b)$]:

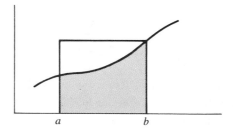

If pairs of points (x, $f(x)$) are generated randomly within the rectangle, the ratio of the number of points that fall beneath the curve to the total number of points generated will equal the ratio of the area under the curve to the area of the rectangle. Write a procedure that uses Monte Carlo integration to compute the area under a curve. Test your procedure by computing the area under the sine between 0 and $\pi/2$. Test the sensitivity of the results to the number of random points that are generated by computing the area from 10 random points, 100 random points, 500 random points, and 1000 random points.

Be sure to think about how to generate random points so that the points are uniformly distributed within the rectangle. Also think about how to tell if a point falls above or below the curve.

Finding Roots of Equations

Storage of ethane in a tank

For a new industrial process, ethane gas, C_2H_6, must be held under high pressure at a low temperature. The crucial factor in the design of the tank for the ethane gas is the relationship among the volume, the temperature, and the amount or mass of gas stored. Under normal conditions, the ideal gas law could be used to find this relationship:

$$PV = nRT \qquad (5.1)$$

where P = the pressure in pa

V = the volume in m^3

n = the number of moles of gas

R = 8.314 pa$-m^3$ mole^{-1} K^{-1}

T = the temperature in Kelvin

But when a gas is at either a high pressure or a low temperature, the assumptions of the ideal gas law are violated. An alternative for the equation of state for a gas is van der Waals' equation:

$$\left(P + a\frac{n^2}{V^2}\right)(V - nb) = nRT \qquad (5.2)$$

In Equation 5.2, the values of the constants a and b depend on the gas. For ethane,

$$a = 0.556 \text{ m}^6\text{pa/mole}^2$$
$$b = 6.38 \times 10^{-5} \text{ m}^3\text{/mole}$$

The current proposed design calls for the tank to have a volume of 300.0 liters and be maintained at a pressure of 2.0×10^7 pascals. Write a generalized Pascal function that can be passed to another subprogram to compute the number of moles in ethane in the tank at any given temperature.

Algorithm development

The solution to the problem requires a value of n that will satisfy Equation 5.2; thus n is a root of the equation. Equation 5.2 can be rewritten as

$$\left(P + a\,\frac{n^2}{V^2}\right)(V - nb) - nRT = 0 \tag{5.3}$$

where a, b, and R are constants and the volume V, the pressure P, and the temperature T are given. This equation is in the form $f(n) = 0$.

Stated in general terms, you are given a function

$$y = f(x)$$

and must find a value of x such that $y = 0$. The values of x that result in $y = 0$ are *roots* of the equation $y = f(x)$. The number of roots of a polynomial equation is the same as the greatest power of x in the equation. However, usually only one root is of interest in equations that are models of physical systems. In the solution to the case study, you are interested in a positive real number that represents the number of moles of ethane in the tank. You are not interested in negative or imaginary roots.

The problem in the case study is to compute the number of moles of ethane gas for any given temperature. You will need to write a Pascal function for Equation 5.3, constants to store the values of a, b, and R, and variables to store the values of **Moles, Pressure, Temperature,** and **Volume.** The major problem is to write the algorithm to find the roots of $y = f(x)$. Algorithm 5.1, which is the first iteration of the algorithm, is necessarily sketchy. The rest of this section will develop a technique for solving Step 2 in Algorithm 5.1.

ALGORITHM 5.1   First iteration of the algorithm for Case Study 5

begin algorithm

    1. Initialize the program
        Request **Temperature, Pressure,** and **Volume** from the user

    2. Find the value of **Moles** such that Equation 5.3 is satisfied

    3. Report the value of **Moles**

end algorithm

Finding roots of equations

The real roots of an equation can sometimes be approximated graphically by plotting the function $f(x)$ and finding the values at which $f(x)$ crosses the x-axis, as shown in Figure 5.1.

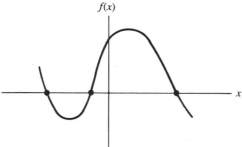

FIGURE 5.1
The roots of $f(x) = \phi y$.

For the most part, however, the roots discovered by this method are not very accurate. For some functions, equations exist that give an exact solution. For example, given an equation in the general form

$$f(x) = ax^2 + bx + c = 0 \qquad (5.4)$$

you can use the quadratic equation to find the roots:

$$x = \frac{-b \pm \sqrt{b^2 - 4ac}}{2a} \qquad (5.5)$$

The values of x found using Equation 5.5 satisfy $f(x) = 0$. Many functions, however, do not have equations that you can use to find the roots. For these functions, numerical techniques must be used.

As stated previously, a root of an equation is a value of x for which $f(x)$ is equal to zero. Of course, the computed value of $f(x)$ is rarely exactly equal to zero. Even with the quadratic formula, which is an exact equation, the value of a function is identically equal to zero only when $b^2 - 4ac$ is a perfect square. Therefore, a criterion is necessary to determine how close to zero $f(x)$ should be before x is called a root. Let x_1 be the candidate for the root of the function $f(x)$. If x is a root of $f(x)$ and if

$$|f(x_1)| \text{ is small} \qquad \text{and} \qquad |x_1 - x| \text{ is small} \qquad (5.6)$$

then x_1 is a root. If, however, only one of these criteria is met, the situation illustrated in either Figure 5.2 or Figure 5.3 could arise.

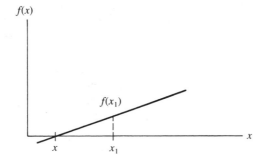

FIGURE 5.2
$|f(x_1)|$ is small, but $|x_1 - x|$ is not small.

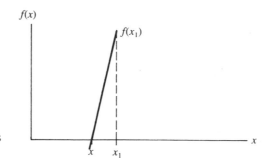

FIGURE 5.3
$|f(x_1)|$ is not small, but $|x_1 - x|$ is small.

An additional problem in using the criteria of Equation 5.6 is that you do not know the true value of the root, x, and therefore in order to measure $|x_1 - x|$ you have to accept as a substitute for x a value, call it x^*, for which $f(x^*)$ is sufficiently close to zero.

What is sufficiently close to zero depends on the problem you are solving and the computer you are using. In writing a program that tests for small differences, the normal practice is to define a constant that is used for testing throughout the program. If your constant is too small, you will never meet the criterion for finding a root and ending the program. You must ensure that the constant you define is not smaller than the rounding error of the computer you are working on. The number $1.0e-50$ is a valid real number, but few current computers store 50 significant digits in a real number. Once the program is running, it may be necessary to fine tune the constant, trading off between the accuracy of the answer and the running time of the program.

In a Pascal program, you could use the statements

```
const  Delta = 1.0e-6;
         .
         .
         .
   if abs (Curve(X)) < Delta then ...
```

to test whether a value of **X** is a root of the curve represented by the Pascal function **Curve.** Notice that if the test were **Curve(X)** < **Delta,** any negative value of **Curve(X)** would pass, so the test is made on the absolute value of **Curve(X).**

Now that you have a criterion for telling whether a value of x is a root, you need to find values to test. One method is to guess a value for x and use the value to compute $f(x)$. If $f(x)$ meets the criterion for a root, then stop; otherwise, guess again. Keep guessing until $f(x)$ meets the criterion. Guessing is the basic technique used in all the algorithms for finding roots, but some ways of guessing are more efficient than others.

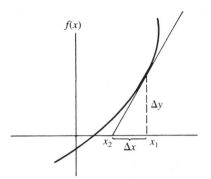

FIGURE 5.4
Generating the second guess using Newton-Raphson.

The Newton-Raphson algorithm for computing roots is a fairly efficient, straightforward way to compute the real roots of an equation. This algorithm uses the derivative of the function $f(x)$ to improve each guess.

If the first guess is x_1, the Newton-Raphson algorithm defines the next value of x to be

$$x_2 = x_1 - \Delta x \tag{5.7}$$

where Δx is chosen so that the second guess, x_2, is closer to the actual value of x than was the first guess, x_1. Figure 5.4 illustrates the method for computing Δx.

In Figure 5.4, the slope of the line tangent to the function $f(x)$ at the point $f(x_1)$ is the derivative of the function at that point. This slope is approximately equal to

$$f'(x_1) \cong \frac{\Delta y}{\Delta x} = \frac{f(x_1)}{\Delta x} \tag{5.8}$$

where $f'(x_1)$ is the derivative of $f(x)$ evaluated at x_1.

Rearranging Equation 5.8 yields an approximation for Δx, or the difference between the first guess and the second guess:

$$\Delta x = \frac{f(x_1)}{f'(x_1)} \tag{5.9}$$

Substituting Equation 5.9 into Equation 5.7 gives

$$x_2 = x_1 - \frac{f(x_1)}{f'(x_1)} \tag{5.10}$$

If x_2 meets the stopping criterion (that is, if $f(x_2) \cong 0$), then x_2 is the root. Otherwise, the process is repeated; x_2 becomes the old guess, and the new guess x_3 is

$$x_3 = x_2 - \frac{f(x_2)}{f'(x_2)} \tag{5.11}$$

Equation 5.11 can be written more generally as

$$x_{n+1} = x_n - \frac{f(x_n)}{f'(x_n)} \tag{5.12}$$

Using the **Derivative** function developed in the application section on numerical differentiation, Equation 5.12 can be written in Pascal as

```
NewX := OldX + (Curve (OldX) / Derivative (Curve, OldX))
```

Three iterations of the Newton-Raphson method are illustrated in Figure 5.5.

The Newton-Raphson algorithm can be used for any equation of the form $y = f(x)$. It will converge to a root as long as the following conditions are met:

1. The initial guess x_1 must be sufficiently close to the root $f(x)=0$. (If the first guess is too far from the root, the approximation $f'(x) = f(x)/\Delta x$ will not be valid.)

2. The first derivative $f'(x)$ must not be close to zero. (If the tangent line is parallel or almost parallel to the x-axis, it will not intersect the x-axis, and Δx will approach infinity.)

3. The second derivative $f''(x)$ must not be too large; that is, the curve cannot be changing too quickly.

Violations of each of these conditions are illustrated in Figure 5.6.

A computer program that finds a root using the Newton-Raphson algorithm should include a test to be sure that conditions 2 and 3 are met.

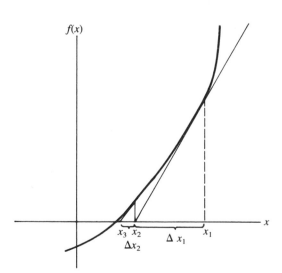

FIGURE 5.5
Three iterations of the
Newton-Raphson algorithm.

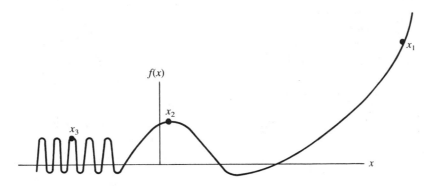

FIGURE 5.6
Violations of the three conditions for Newton-Raphson: x_1 violates condition 1, x_2 violates condition 2, and x_3 violates condition 3.

Otherwise, execution of the program may end in a run-time error because division by zero was attempted. Worse, the program may be caught in an infinite loop as the values for x swing from minus infinity to plus infinity. Because of inherent numerical errors, there is no guarantee that a function actually meets the criteria even if the function passes the tests.

Any time you write a program that uses an iterative technique, such as the Newton-Raphson, you should keep track of the number of iterations. After every 100 or so iterations, write a message to the user stating the cumulative number of iterations and the current values of the important variables. You should give the user the options of continuing the program, stopping the program, or starting over. Algorithm 5.2 is an algorithm for the Newton-Raphson technique.

ALGORITHM 5.2   Algorithm for the Newton-Raphson technique

begin algorithm
1. Initialize the variables
     IterationNumber ← 0
2. Read the initial data
     a. Request the value of **Y**
     b. Request the first guess **X1**
     c. Check the first condition, that **X1** be close to the true root
         i. Evaluate $f(\mathbf{X1})$
         ii. Report $f(\mathbf{X1})$ and $\mathbf{Y} - f(\mathbf{X1})$
         iii. Ask the user if a new initial guess is required

3. Find the root
  OldX ← **X1**
  repeat
   a. **IterationNumber** ← **IterationNumber** + 1
   b. if **IterationNumber** > **TooManyIterations** then
    RequestHelpFromUser
   c. Check the second two conditions
    i. if abs(f'(**OldX**)) < **Small** then **Error** ← **true**
    ii. if abs(f''(**OldX**)) > **Large** then **Error** ← **true**
   d. If not (**Error**), then compute **NewX**
    NewX ← **OldX** + f(**OldX**) / f'(**OldX**)
   e. Check if **NewX** is a root; if not, get ready for the next
    iteration
    if abs(f(**NewX**)) < **Small** and
     abs(**NewX** − **OldX**) < **Small** then
     Done ← **true**
    else
     OldX ← **NewX**
  until **Done** or **Error**
4. Return the results
  if not (**Error**), then the function value is **NewRoot**
  else
  report the error condition
end algorithm

Algorithm 5.2 can be used to write a Pascal procedure that finds a root of a function in the general form $y = f(x)$. The procedure **NewtonR** has a function in its parameter list allowing any single-valued real function to be passed into it. **NewtonR** also invokes function **YesEntered,** which was developed in Chapter 6 of the main text. It also uses the previously developed functions **Derivative** and **SecondDerivative** to evaluate $f'(x)$ and $f''(x)$.

```
procedure NewtonR (function F (Z : real): real; var Y, Root : real;
                   var Flag : boolean);
(*      NewtonR is an interactive procedure that finds a root of the       *)
(*      function F, using the Newton-Raphson algorithm.  Flag returns      *)
(*      with a value of true if a root cannot be found or the user         *)
(*      requests to stop.                                                  *)

const Small = 1.0e-06;              (* constant to test small values. *)
      Large = 1.0e20;              (* constant to test large values. *)
      TooManyIterations = 50;      (* to compare to the number of *)
                                   (* iterations. *)
var   NoRoot : boolean;            (* flag set to true if no root can be *)
                                   (* found. *)
      NoMore : boolean;            (* flag set to true when the user *)
                                   (* user requests to stop. *)
```

```
(*$i derivative *)
(*$i secondderivative *)
(*$i yesentered *)


  procedure Initialize;
  (*     This procedure writes the initial message to the terminal.          *)

  begin
    writeln;
    writeln (' This procedure finds a root of a function in the form');
    writeln (' y = f(x).  The function f(x) is passed to the procedure as');
    writeln (' F(X).  You will be asked to enter the first guess for x.');
    writeln;
  end; (* procedure Initialize *)

  procedure ReadInitialValues(var RightHandSide, X : real);
  (*     ReadInitialValues reads the value of y and the first guess          *)
  (*     from the terminal.  The value of F(firstguess) is reported to       *)
  (*     allow the user to make another guess if the first guess is          *)
  (*     not good.  This procedure uses a recursive version of               *)
  (*     YesEntered to test if a yes was entered from the terminal.          *)

  var  FirstY : real;       (* local variable to store the value of *)
                            (* F(firstguess). *)

  begin
    repeat
      writeln (' What is your guess for the value of X such that F(X) = Y?');
      readln (X);

      FirstY := F(X);

      writeln (' For X = ',X:10:2,' F(X) = ',FirstY:10:2);
      writeln (' Y - F(X) =',(RightHandSide - F(X)):12:4);
      writeln;
      writeln (' Do you want to enter another value for X?');
    until not (YesEntered)
  end; (* procedure ReadInitialValues *)


  procedure RequestHelpFromUser (var IterNo : integer; var NewX, OldX : real;
                            var RequestToStop : boolean);
  (*     This procedure is called when too many iterations have been          *)
  (*     performed.  It prints the current values and allows the user         *)
  (*     to make a new guess for x or to stop the program.                    *)
```

```
begin
  writeln;
  writeln (' There have been ', IterNo:1, ' iterations');
  writeln (' The values for ', (IterNo - 1):1, ' were:  X =', OldX,
           ' and F(X) =', F (OldX));
  writeln (' The values for ', IterNo:1, ' were:  X =', NewX, ' and',
           ' F(X) =', F(NewX));
  writeln;
  writeln (' Do you want to enter a new guess for X?');
  writeln (' Enter ''y'' if you want to enter a new value');
  writeln (' Enter ''n'' to stop the program');
  if YesEntered then
    begin
      IterNo := 0;
      writeln (' Enter a new value for X');
      readln (NewX)
    end
  else
    RequestToStop := true
end; (* procedure RequestHelpFromUser *)

procedure FindTheRoot (RightHandSide : real; var NewX : real;
                       var Error, RequestToStop : boolean);
(*       This procedure uses the Newton-Raphson algorithm to find the     *)
(*       root of the equation F(X).                                       *)

var    IterNo : integer;       (* number of iterations so far. *)
       OldX : real;            (* value of X at IterNo -1. *)
       Done : boolean;         (* boolean flag --set to true when the root *)
                               (* is found. *)

begin
  Done := false;              (* set all the flags to false. *)
  Error := false;
  RequestToStop := false;
  IterNo := 0;

  repeat
    OldX := NewX;

    (* Test if the values of the derivatives are too small or too large *)
    (* the Newton-Raphson algorithm to work correctly. *)

    if abs (Derivative (F, OldX) ) < Small then Error := true;
    if abs (SecondDerivative (F, OldX)) > Large then Error := true;

    (* If both tests are passed, then compute the next value of X. *)
```

```
    if not (Error) then
      begin
        NewX := OldX - (F (OldX) - RightHandSide) / Derivative (F, OldX);

        if (abs (F (NewX) - RightHandSide) < Small )
            and (abs (NewX - OldX) < Small) then
          Done := true
      end;  (* if not error *)

    IterNo := IterNo + 1;
    if not (Done) and (IterNo > TooManyIterations) then
       RequestHelpFromUser (IterNo, NewX, OldX, RequestToStop)
  until Done or Error or RequestToStop
end; (* procedure FindTheRoot *)

  procedure ReportStop (Error, RequestToStop : boolean);
  (*     This procedure writes the message if the procedure ends with-    *)
  (*     out finding a root.                                              *)

  begin
    if Error then
      writeln (' A root cannot be found.');
    if RequestToStop then
      writeln (' Procedure Newton-Raphson stopping.')
  end; (* procedure ReportStop *)


begin (* main body of procedure NewtonR *)
  NoRoot := false;

  Initialize;
  ReadInitialValues (Y, Root);

  FindTheRoot (Y, Root, NoRoot, NoMore);

  ReportStop (NoRoot, NoMore);
  if NoRoot or NoMore then
    Flag := true
  else
    Flag := false
end; (* procedure NewtonR *)
```

Solution to Case Study 5

Now that the procedure **NewtonR** has been developed, the solution to the case study is almost complete. Only the input/output procedures are needed. The program **MolesOfEthane** uses the functions **NewtonR, Derivative,** and **SecondDerivative** to compute the number of moles of ethane gas in a tank under a constant pressure for any user-specified temperature.

PROGRAM 5.1   MolesOfEthane

```
program MolesOfEthane (input, output);
(*      This program uses Newton-Raphson to find the moles of ethane      *)
(*      in a tank of a given volume and under a given pressure.           *)

var   Temperature : real;           (* temperature in Kelvin. *)
      Moles : real;                 (* number of moles of gas. *)
      Flag : boolean;               (* flag from Newton-Raphson - set to *)
                                    (* true if no root is found. *)

  function Kelvin (Mols : real) : real;
      (*      Function Kelvin returns the temperature in Kelvin given the  *)
      (*      number of moles of gas using van der Waals' equation.        *)
      (*      (Equation 15.26).                                            *)

  const A = 0.556;            (* meters**6-pascals per mole**2. *)
        B = 6.38e-05;         (* meters**3 per mole. *)
        R = 8.314;            (* universal gas constant in pascal- *)
                              (* meter**3 per mole per Kelvin. *)
        Pressure = 2.0e07;    (* pressure in pascals. *)
        Volume =300.e-03;     (* volume of gas in meters cubed. *)

  begin
    Kelvin := (Pressure + A * sqr (Mols / Volume)) * (Volume - Mols * B) /
                (Mols * R)
  end; (* function Kelvin *)


(*$i newtonr *)
```

```
(*------------------------------------------------------------------*)
begin (* main *)
  writeln (' This program finds the moles of methane in a tank.  The tank ');
  writeln (' has constant volume and is maintained at a constant pressure.');
  writeln (' What is the temperature in the tank?');
  readln (Temperature);
  writeln;
  writeln (' In the Newton-Raphson procedure, X is the number of moles');
  writeln (' in Kelvin and Y is the temperature.');

  NewtonR (Kelvin, Temperature, Moles, Flag);

  if not Flag then
    begin
      writeln;
      writeln (' When the temperature in the tank', Temperature:10:2,
               ' degrees Kelvin,');
      writeln (' the number of moles is ', Moles:10:2)
    end;
  writeln
end.  (* program MolesOfEthane *)

=>
 This program finds the moles of methane in a tank.  The tank
 has constant volume and is maintained at a constant pressure.
 What is the temperature in the tank?
□300.0

 In the Newton-Raphson procedure, X is the number of moles
 in Kelvin and Y is the temperature.

 This procedure finds a root of a function in the form
 y = f(x).  The function f(x) is passed to the procedure as
 F(X).  You will be asked to enter the first guess for x.

 What is your guess for the value of X such that F(X) = Y?
□500
 For X =      500.00 F(X) =      1389.48
 Y - F(X) =  -1089.4793

 Do you want to enter another value for X?
 Answer yes or no (y/n)
□n

 When the temperature in the tank     300.00 degrees Kelvin,
 the number of moles is     3199.56
```

Problems

1. Write a general procedure that uses a binary search to find the root of a function. (See Chapter 11 for a description of the binary search.) The function should be in the parameter list of the procedure. Use this procedure in a program to evaluate the cube root of a number. Find the value of x such that

$$f(x) = x^3 - y = 0$$

2. A circuit with a battery that supplies a voltage v_B is connected in series with a resistance R and a solid-state semiconductor diode. The diode, represented by the triangle, essentially allows current to flow only in the direction in which the triangle points:

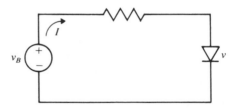

The current I through the diode is given by

$$I = i_s(e^{Cv} - 1)$$

where v = the voltage across the diode in volts

i_s = the reverse saturation current, or bias current, in amperes. This is the maximum current that flows when a large negative voltage is applied to the diode. Under these conditions, the diode is overwhelmed and a current flows in the opposite direction.

C = a constant equal to the charge of an electron divided by the Boltzmann constant times room temperature in Kelvin

= 40 coulomb per joule

The battery voltage v_B can be found by applying Kirchoff's law for the voltage drop around the loop:

$$v_B = IR + v$$

The bias current can be written as a function of the voltage by combining the two preceding equations:

$$i_s = \frac{v_B - v}{(e^{Cv} - 1)R}$$

Given the voltage v, the bias current i_s is easy to find since the values for v_B, C, and R are all known; however, given the bias current, the value of the voltage cannot be found by direct substitution.

Write a program that uses the Newton-Raphson procedure to find the voltage given the bias current. Test your program using $v_B = 20$ V, $R = 50$ Ω, and $i_s = 10^{-9}$ A.

3. The function

$$f(x) = ax^3 + bx^2 + cx + d$$

may have both real and imaginary roots. Write a new version of the Newton-Raphson procedure that finds both real and imaginary roots. Test your procedure by finding the roots of the equation $x^2 + x^4 = 0$.

4. Another method of finding the roots of equations is called *regula falsa,* or the method of false positions. The algorithm for regula falsa is as follows:

   a. Find two values of x such that $f(x_1) < 0$ and $f(x_2) > 0$. Because one value is above zero and the other value is below zero, there must be at least one value of x between x_1 and x_2 for which $f(x)$ is exactly equal to zero. In other words, a root of the equation must lie between x_1 and x_2.

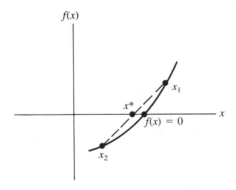

   b. Approximate the value of the root by linear interpolation. Call the resulting value x^*.

   c. Determine whether x^* is a root. It is a root if $|f(x^*)|$ and $|x_1 - x_2|$ are small.

   d. If x^* is not a root, determine whether the root lies in the interval between x_1 and x^* or in the interval between x_2 and x^*. This determination can be made by testing the sign of $f(x^*)f(x_1)$ and the sign of $f(x^*)f(x_2)$.

   (i) If $f(x^*)f(x_1) < 0$, the root lies between x_1 and x^*. Set x_2 to x^*.
   (ii) If $f(x^*)f(x_2) < 0$, the root lies between x_2 and x^*. Set x_1 to x^*.

Repeat steps b through d until a root is found.

Write a general procedure to find a root using *regula falsa.* Use this procedure to solve the following problem:

Suppose you need to borrow $5,000.00 to help pay for your college education. You can afford to pay back $250.00 per month, and you would like to pay it back as quickly as possible. The monthly payment x on a loan can be computed from the formula:

$$x = \frac{(r/12)P(1.0 + r/12)^{12n}}{(1.0 + r/12)^{12n} - 1.0}$$

where r = the interest rate in hundredths (for a 12-percent loan, $r = 0.12$)

P = the principal

n = the number of years of the loan

Solve for n given that the principal is \$5,000.00, the monthly payment is \$250.00, and the rate is 12 percent.

APPLICATION 6
Quick Sort

The quick sort is a recursive sorting algorithm that is faster and more efficient than the algorithms described previously. A recursive algorithm is one in which each step is defined in terms of a previous step. Recursion is discussed in Chapter 15 of the main text. To understand the quick sort, you should be familiar with recursion.

CASE STUDY 6
Sorting power plants

Another user of the program that was developed for Case Studies 18 and 19 in the main text would like an output report of the names of the power plants arranged in descending order by their megawatt power rating. The plants must be sorted by power rating before the report is printed. Write a Pascal procedure that will allow the user to sort the power plants in descending order of their megawatt capacity.

Algorithm development

Again, the main program for the case study exists and the problem is to modify it to meet another user's needs. Given the plant names in random order, how can you sort them in order of decreasing capacity? In the solution to the case study, a test program will be written to compare the three algorithms to sort the data.

So that the algorithms will be understandable, the following numbers will be used for each of the examples. The numbers are stored in an array called **Capacity,** which is of type **IntArray.**

250	750	50	1500	100	500	850	1000	1225

The procedure **Exchange** which was developed in Chapter 6 and which exchanges the integer values stored in array locations **First** and **Second** is used in two of the sorting solutions:

```
procedure Exchange (var First, Second : integer);
(*       Exchange puts the variable that is passed in First into Second      *)
(*       and the variable that is passed in Second into First, using a       *)
(*       temporary variable.                                                 *)

var   Temp : integer;        (* temporary variable to hold value of First *)
                             (* during the exchange. *)

begin
  Temp := First;
  First := Second;
  Second := Temp
end;  (* procedure Exchange *)
```

For example,

```
Exchange (Capacity[8], Capacity[9])
```

would result in the array

250	750	50	1500	100	500	850	1225	1000

Quick Sort

In a quick sort, one element is designated as the pivot element. The array is divided in half by the pivot. The "halves" may or may not be equal. The array is sorted by moving all the elements that are greater than the pivot to the top of the array and all the elements that are less than the pivot to the bottom of the array. New pivots are then selected for each of the original halves of the array. The same process is repeated for each of the halves until the array is sorted.

The first pass through the quick sort works as follows:

1. Set **Low** to the smallest array index, in this case 1.

2. Set **High** to the last array index. For the example, **High** is 9.

3. If **Low** < **High** then

   a. Set the low counter, **I,** to **Low.**

   b. Set the high counter, **J,** to **High.**

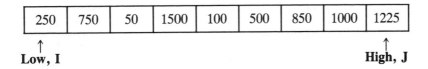

   c. Set the pivot element equal to the value stored in element **High.** (**Pivot** = 1225).

   d. Starting at **Low,** advance the counter, **I,** through the array until the number it points to is less than the capacity of **Pivot,** or until **I** meets **J**:

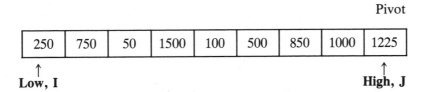

   For this array, **I** does not move because it is pointing at a value that is less than the pivot value.

   e. Decrement **J** through the array until the value it points to is greater than **Pivot** or until **J** meets **I**:

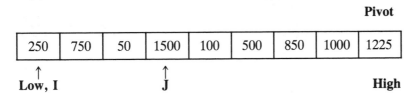

   f. If **I** < **J,** then the elements are out of order, so exchange them.

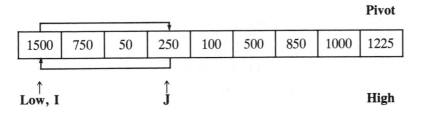

g. Repeat Steps d through f until **I** ≥ **J.**
In the second repetition of Step d, the counter I advances until the element it indicates is less than the pivot element:

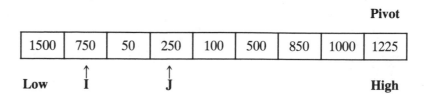

In the second repetition of Step e, the counter **J** moves until it reaches the first value that is greater than **Pivot,** or until it meets **I:**

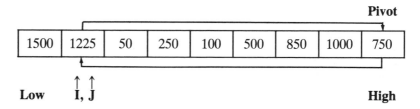

Since **I** is now equal to **J,** the repetition stops.

4. The next step is to exchange the value of **Capacity[I]** with the value of **Capacity[High]:**

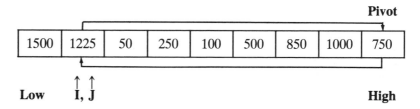

What Steps 1 through 4 have done is to divide the array into two parts: the top part contains all the elements that are greater than or equal to the pivot element (1225), and the bottom part contains all the elements that are less than the pivot element. The essence of the quick-sort algorithm is to then divide each part in two, with one "half" being greater than the new pivot element and the other "half" being less than the new pivot element. In the example, the top part of the array is in order and would remain unchanged for the rest of the sort. For the bottom part, the steps would be repeated:

1. Set **Low** to the smallest array index, in this case 3.

2. Set **High** to the last array index. For the example, **High** is 9.

3. If **Low** < **High** then

   a. Set the low counter, **I,** to **Low.**

   b. Set the high counter, **J,** to **High.**

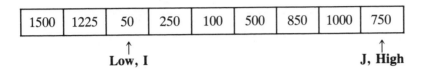

   c. Set the pivot element equal to the value stored in element **High** (**Pivot** = 750).

   d. Starting at **Low,** advance the counter, **I,** through the array until the number it points to is less than the value of **Pivot,** or until **I** meets **J:**

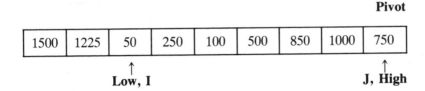

For this array, **I** does not move because it is pointing to a value that is less than the pivot value.

   e. Decrement **J** through the array until the capacity it points to is greater than **Pivot** or until **J** meets **I:**

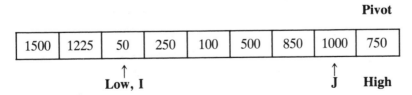

J moves until it points at 1000, the first value that is greater than **Pivot.**

   f. If **I** < **J,** the elements are out of order, so exchange them.

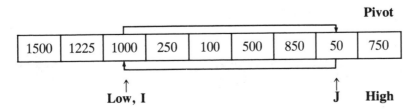

g. Repeat Steps d through f until **I** ≥ **J.** In the second repetition of Step e, the counter **I** advances until the element it indicates is less than **Pivot:**

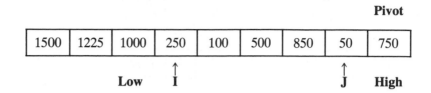

In the second repetition of step e, the counter **J** moves to 850, the first value that is greater than **Pivot:**

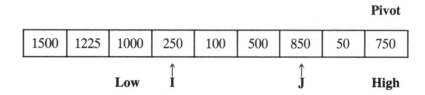

The value of **Capacity[I]** is exchanged with the value of **Capacity[J]:**

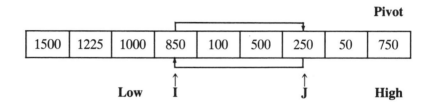

On the third pass through the array, **I** moves down to 100, the first value that is less than **Pivot:**

1500	1225	1000	850	100	500	250	50	750

Pivot

Low   **I**   **J**   **High**

And **J** moves until it equals **I,** since none of the intervening values are greater than **Pivot:**

Pivot

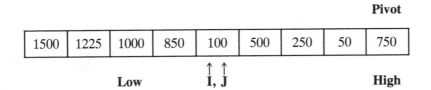

| 1500 | 1225 | 1000 | 850 | 100 | 500 | 250 | 50 | 750 |

Low   ↑ ↑   **High**
                   I, J

4. The next step is to exchange the value of **Capacity[I]** with the value of **Capacity[High]**:

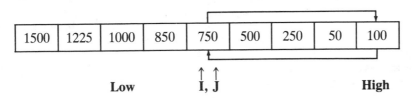

| 1500 | 1225 | 1000 | 850 | 750 | 500 | 250 | 50 | 100 |

Low   ↑ ↑   **High**
                   I, J

The array is now divided into two parts, with all the values greater than or equal to 750 on one side and all the values less than 750 on the other side.

Steps 1 through 4 are repeated until the array is in order. Although the quick sort is difficult to explain, it is very efficient. In the worst case, when the array is already in order, the quick sort makes n^2 comparisons and exchanges. In the best case, when the array is completely out of order, the quick sort makes approximately $n \log (n)$ comparisons and exchanges. The recursive algorithm for the quick sort is coded in Pascal as

```
procedure QuickSort (ArrayLimit: integer; var SortArray : IntArray);
(*      QuickSort is a recursive procedure that uses an algorithm          *)
(*      developed by C.A.R. Hoare.                                         *)

  procedure RecurseQuick (Low, High : integer);

  var   I, J : integer;        (* locations of the low and high counters. *)
        Pivot : integer;       (* at each pass, the array is split in two *)
                               (* parts, with one part greater than Pivot *)
                               (* and one part less than Pivot. *)
  begin
    if Low < High then
      begin
        I := Low;
        J := High;
        Pivot := SortArray[J];
```

```
        repeat
          while (I < J)  and (SortArray[I] >= Pivot) do I := I + 1;
          while (I < J)  and (SortArray[J] <= Pivot) do J := J - 1;

          if (I < J) then       (* if I < J, the elements are out of order. *)
            Exchange (SortArray[I], SortArray[J])
        until (I >= J);

        Exchange (SortArray[I], SortArray[High]);    (* move the pivot *)
                                                     (* element to I. *)

        if (I - Low > High - I) then       (* Test whether array is now in *)
                                           (* order. If it is not in order, *)
                                           (* invoke procedure RecurseQuick *)
                                           (* from inside itself. *)

          begin
            RecurseQuick (Low, I - 1);
            RecurseQuick (I + 1, High)
          end
        else
          begin
            RecurseQuick (I + 1, High);
            RecurseQuick (Low, I - 1)
          end
      end (* if Low < High *)
  end; (* procedure RecurseQuick *)

begin (* procedure QuickSort *)
  RecurseQuick (1, ArrayLimit)
end; (* procedure QuickSort *)
```

Solution to Case Study 6

Four algorithms have been developed for sorting the power plants. Any one of the sorting procedures can be added to the program and will allow the user to sort the plant names by megawatt power rating.

In order to show you how the different algorithms compare in efficiency, we modified the procedures **SelectSort, BubbleSort, Insertion-Sort,** and **QuickSort** so that the numbers of comparisons, exchanges, and assignment statements were counted. The output below is from a test program that executed each of the procedures. Each sort algorithm was executed with the original unordered data.

```
The initial order of the array for each sort is:
  250    750    50  1500   100   500   850  1000  1225
```

```
For the selection sort,
the number of exchanges was 8,
the number of comparisons was 44, and
the number of assignments was 22.

The final order of the array is:
  1500  1225  1000   850   750   500   250   100    50

For the bubble sort,
the number of exchanges was 26,
the number of comparisons was 52, and
the number of assignments was 52.

The final order of the array is:
  1500  1225  1000   850   750   500   250   100    50

For the insertion sort,
the number of exchanges was 0,
the number of comparisons was 52, and
the number of assignments was 77.

The final order of the array is:
  1500  1225  1000   850   750   500   250   100    50

For the quick sort,
the number of exchanges was 8,
the number of comparisons was 73, and
the number of assignments was 19.
The number of calls to RecurseQuick was 6682

The final order of the array is:
  1500  1225  1000   850   750   500   250   100    50
```

Problems

1. Write a program that sorts the persons in the following list into alphabetical order and then sorts them into numerical order by ID using the quick sort.

Byron, Ada	123456789	Zeppelin, Ferdinand	987654321
Edison, Thomas A.	234567890	Diesel, Rudolph	098765432
Euclid	345678901	Bohr, Niels	109876543
Pascal, Blaise	456789012	Ampere, Andre	210987654
Boole, George	567890123	Volta, Count	321098765
Einstein, Albert	678901234	Faraday, Michael	432109876
Copernicus, Nicholas	789012345	Fahrenheit, Gabriel	543210987
Kepler, Johannes	890123456	Maxwell, James C	654321098
Curie, Marie	901234567	Newton, Sir Isaac	765432109
LaGrange, Pierre S	012345678	daVinci, Leonardo	876543210

2. Using the heights and weights of the persons in the following list, write a program to print three lists of students: one in alphabetical order, one from lightest to heaviest, and one from tallest to shortest.

	Feet	Inches	Pounds
Pascal	6	2	160
Curie	5	1	110
Milton	5	8	135
Gauss	5	10	200
Anthony	5	3	115

Determinants of Matrices

The *determinant* is a single scalar value created by combining the elements of a matrix in an arbitrarily defined fashion. In the early eighteenth century, when linear algebra was a new topic, mathematicians hoped that the determinant could be used to represent an entire matrix and thus eliminate some tedious matrix operations. The determinant has proved to be less powerful than originally anticipated, but it is still useful in many algorithms.

In this section, you will learn how to find the determinant of a matrix and to use the determinant to ascertain whether a unique solution exists for a system of linear equations. The problem in Case Study 7 will be formulated using matrix notation that will be used also in Case Study 8, in which the solution to the system of equations will be found.

CASE STUDY 7
Three-loop circuit

A three-loop direct-current (DC) circuit with two voltage sources and four resistors has been wired as shown in Figure 7.1. The equations that describe the current in each loop must be derived in order to find the current flowing through each loop in the circuit. Ohm's law gives the voltage across a resistor as a function of the current:

$$V = IR \qquad (7.1)$$

where V = voltage in volts (V)

I = current in amperes (A)

R = resistance in ohms (Ω)

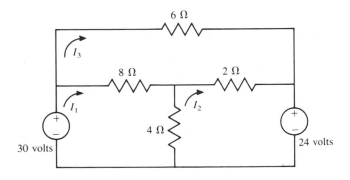

FIGURE 7.1
Currents in a three-loop DC circuit.

For the loop on the lower left in Figure 7.1, the voltage across the 8Ω resistor is $8I_1$ and the voltage across the 4Ω resistor is $4(I_1 - I_2)$, where I_1 is the current flowing in the loop on the left and I_2 is the current flowing in the loop on the right. Notice that the direction of the current flow is important. In the figure, both I_1 and I_2 are defined to be positive in the clockwise direction, so the currents flow in opposite directions through the 4Ω resistor.

Ohm's law gives only the voltage across a resistor; Kirchoff's law is needed to find the current in the loop. Kirchoff's law states that the voltage around any closed loop in a circuit equals zero. Combining Ohm's law with Kirchoff's law yields an equation for the current in each loop. Adding the voltages in the lower left-hand loop in a clockwise direction results in the following circuit equation:

$$8I_1 + 4(I_1 - I_2) - 8I_3 - 30 = 0$$

or   (7.2)

$$12I_1 - 4I_2 - 8I_3 - 30 = 0$$

Notice that the clockwise direction of current results in the addition of -30 volts, since by definition positive current flows from positive to negative.

Similarly, you can use Ohm's law to compute the voltage across each of the resistors in the lower right-hand loop. Then, using Kirchoff's law, you can write the equation for the right-hand loop:

$$4(I_2 - I_1) + 2(I_2 - I_3) + 24 = 0 \qquad (7.3)$$

Finally, the equation for the upper loop is

$$8(I_3 - I_1) + 6I_3 + 2(I_3 - I_2) = 0 \qquad (7.4)$$

Equations 7.2 through 7.4 form a system of simultaneous linear equations:

$$\begin{aligned}
12I_1 - 4I_2 - 8I_3 &= 30 \\
-4I_1 + 6I_2 - 2I_3 &= -24 \\
-8I_1 - 2I_2 + 16I_3 &= 0
\end{aligned}$$

In standard notation I represents the identity matrix, so in the remainder of the section the currents will be represented by x rather than I. The system of equations is now written as

$$\begin{aligned}
12x_1 - 4x_2 - 8x_3 &= 30 \\
-4x_1 + 6x_2 - 2x_3 &= -24 \\
-8x_1 - 2x_2 + 16x_3 &= 0
\end{aligned} \qquad (7.5)$$

The values of x_1, x_2, and x_3 that satisfy all three equations simultaneously solve the circuit problem.

Write a program that determines whether there is a unique solution for the electrical current flowing in each loop of the circuit.

Algorithm development

Knowing simply that a test can be performed on the determinant to indicate whether a unique solution exists, you can write a preliminary version of the algorithm. Algorithm 7.1 assumes that there is sufficient information in the diagram to compute the determinant.

If the voltages and resistances are entered, additional information about the wiring of the circuit will be required to derive the equations for each loop. An algorithm to request this information from the user and then to compute the coefficients for the equations would be difficult to write. Therefore, you can assume that the user has done the analysis, and you can request the coefficients of the matrix rather than the voltages and resistances.

ALGORITHM 7.1   First iteration for the solution to Case Study 7

begin algorithm
1. Read the coefficient matrix **Coeff** for the equations that have been derived from the voltages and resistances
2. Compute the **Determinant**
3. Test the **Determinant**
    if a solution exists then
        write 'A solution for the circuit exists, and the solution is unique.'
    else
        write 'A unique solution for the circuit does not exist.'
end algorithm

Matrix form of linear equations

The first step in finding a solution to the problem in Case Study 7 is to rewrite the equations in a generalized *matrix form:*

$$Ax = b \tag{7.6}$$

where A is the square matrix of equation coefficients, that is, the *coefficient matrix,* b is the column vector of the right-hand sides or constant terms of the equations, and x is the column vector of unknown currents. Equation 7.5 can be written in the form of Equation 7.6 by writing the matrix A and vector b for Equations 7.5. For the case study, you must determine whether values for the vector x that satisfy Equation 7.7 exist and whether the values are unique.

$$\overset{\mathbf{A}}{\begin{bmatrix} 12 & -4 & -8 \\ -4 & 6 & -2 \\ -8 & -2 & 16 \end{bmatrix}} \overset{\mathbf{x}}{\begin{bmatrix} x_1 \\ x_2 \\ x_3 \end{bmatrix}} = \overset{\mathbf{B}}{\begin{bmatrix} 30 \\ -24 \\ 0 \end{bmatrix}} \tag{7.7}$$

The formula for the determinant

The general formula for the determinant of an n by n matrix is complicated, so the first part of this discussion is limited to 2 by 2 and 3 by 3 matrices. The last topic in this section is a general formula for the determinant.

If A is the 2 by 2 matrix

$$\begin{bmatrix} a_{11} & a_{12} \\ a_{21} & a_{22} \end{bmatrix}$$

then the determinant of A is defined to be

$$\det A = a_{11}a_{22} - a_{12}a_{21} \tag{7.8}$$

If A is the 3 by 3 matrix

$$\begin{bmatrix} a_{11} & a_{12} & a_{13} \\ a_{21} & a_{22} & a_{23} \\ a_{31} & a_{32} & a_{33} \end{bmatrix}$$

the determinant of A is defined as

$$\det A = + a_{11}a_{22}a_{33} + a_{12}a_{23}a_{31} + a_{13}a_{21}a_{32} \\ - a_{11}a_{23}a_{32} - a_{12}a_{21}a_{33} - a_{13}a_{22}a_{31} \tag{7.9}$$

Equation 7.9 can be used to write a Pascal function for the determinant of a 3 by 3 matrix. A function, rather than a procedure, is appropriate because the determinant is a single scalar value. An array data type is required so that the matrix can be passed in the parameter list.

```
const MaxRows = 3;        (* maximum number of equations - that is, rows *)
                          (* in the matrix. *)
      MaxColumns = 3;     (* maximum number of variables - that is, *)
                          (* columns in the matrix. *)

type  Matrix = array [1.. MaxRows, 1..MaxColumns] of real;
```

The function for the determinant can be written directly from Equation 7.9:

```
function Determinant3 (A : Matrix) : real;
(*     The function Determinant3 returns the determinant of the three    *)
(*     by three matrix A.                                                *)

begin
  Determinant3 :=   A[1,1] * A[2,2] * A[3,3] + A[1,2] * A[2,3] * A[3,1]
                  + A[1,3] * A[2,1] * A[3,2] - A[1,1] * A[2,3] * A[3,2]
                  - A[1,2] * A[2,1] * A[3,3] - A[1,3] * A[2,2] * A[3,1]
end; (* function Determinant3 *)
```

Note that the function **Determinant3** works only for 3 by 3 matrices. How could you make the same function work for both 2 by 2 and 3 by 3 matrices?

Some properties of determinants

The determinant of a matrix has many properties that can be used in solving problems using matrices. In the following list of some of the properties of determinants, each property is illustrated using a 2 by 2 matrix. The illustrations, however, are not proofs. The following properties hold for any n by n matrix, but you cannot assume that any property you can demonstrate using a 2 by 2 matrix is thereby proven for all matrices.

1. If a matrix is scaled by a constant,

$$A' = cA$$

the determinant is also scaled by the constant.

$$\det A' = \det (cA) = c \det A$$

$$\det \begin{bmatrix} ca_{11} & ca_{12} \\ ca_{21} & ca_{22} \end{bmatrix} = c \det \begin{bmatrix} a_{11} & a_{12} \\ a_{21} & a_{22} \end{bmatrix}$$

$$ca_{11}ca_{22} - ca_{12}ca_{21} = c \, (a_{11}a_{22} - a_{12}a_{21})$$

2. If two rows of a matrix are interchanged, the sign of the determinant changes.

$$\det \begin{bmatrix} a_{11} & a_{12} \\ a_{21} & a_{22} \end{bmatrix} = - \det \begin{bmatrix} a_{21} & a_{22} \\ a_{11} & a_{12} \end{bmatrix}$$

$$a_{11}a_{22} - a_{12}a_{21} = -(a_{21}a_{12} - a_{22}a_{11})$$

3. If two columns of a matrix are interchanged, the sign of the determinant changes.

$$\det \begin{bmatrix} a_{11} & a_{12} \\ a_{21} & a_{22} \end{bmatrix} = - \det \begin{bmatrix} a_{12} & a_{11} \\ a_{22} & a_{21} \end{bmatrix}$$

$$a_{11}a_{22} - a_{12}a_{21} = -(a_{12}a_{21} - a_{11}a_{22})$$

4. If two rows of a matrix are equal, the determinant of A is equal to 0.

$$\det \begin{bmatrix} a_{11} & a_{12} \\ a_{11} & a_{12} \end{bmatrix} = a_{11}a_{12} - a_{12}a_{11} = 0$$

5. The determinant of the product of any two n by n matrices is the product of their determinants.

$$(\det A)(\det B) = \det AB$$

$$\det \begin{bmatrix} a_{11} & a_{12} \\ a_{21} & a_{22} \end{bmatrix} \det \begin{bmatrix} b_{11} & b_{12} \\ b_{21} & b_{22} \end{bmatrix} = \det \begin{bmatrix} a_{11}b_{11} + a_{12}b_{21} & a_{11}b_{12} + a_{12}b_{22} \\ a_{21}b_{11} + a_{22}b_{21} & a_{21}b_{12} + a_{22}b_{22} \end{bmatrix}$$

$$(a_{11}a_{22} - a_{12}a_{21})(b_{11}b_{22} - b_{12}b_{21}) = \begin{aligned} &(a_{11}b_{11} + a_{12}b_{21})(a_{21}b_{12} + a_{22}b_{22}) \\ &- (a_{11}b_{12} + a_{12}b_{22})(a_{21}b_{11} + a_{22}b_{21}) \end{aligned}$$

Overdetermined and underdetermined matrices

Some sets of simultaneous equations cannot be solved because they have either an infinite number of solutions or no solution. If the number of solutions is infinite, the equations are said to be *underdetermined*. If there is no solution, the equations are said to be *overdetermined*. Because overdetermined and underdetermined systems of equations do not have solutions, it is useful to have a method for identifying them prior to attempting to solve them.

An underdetermined system of equations arises when there are more unknowns than equations or when two or more equations are multiples of each other. Two equations that are multiples of each other are called *linearly dependent* equations. The following system of equations is underdetermined because the equations are linearly dependent:

$$\begin{aligned} y + 4z &= 2 \\ 3y + 12z &= 6 \end{aligned} \tag{7.10}$$

The number of values for y and z that satisfy both equations is infinite. All values of y and z that lie on the line $z = -\frac{1}{4}y + \frac{1}{2}$ satisfy both equations. Because the two equations are equivalent, there is essentially one equation with two unknowns. Similarly, the system of equations

$$\begin{aligned} a + 4b + c &= 2 \\ 3a + 2b - c &= 100 \end{aligned} \tag{7.11}$$

is underdetermined because the number of values of a, b, and c that satisfy the two equations is infinite. Each equation represent a plane, and all the points that lie in the intersection of the two planes satisfy both equations.

An underdetermined system can be identified by the value of the determinant of the coefficient matrix. If an infinite number of solutions to a set of equations exist, the determinant of the matrix will be equal to zero. To confirm that the coefficient matrix of an underdetermined system has a determinant of zero, compute the determinant of the matrix for Equations 7.10:

$$\det \begin{bmatrix} 1 & 4 \\ 3 & 12 \end{bmatrix} = 12 - 12 = 0 \tag{7.12}$$

A matrix with a determinant of zero is called a *singular matrix*.

Before matrix manipulations are begun, the determinant should be checked to be sure that it is not equal to zero. However, this test is not necessarily straightforward to perform on a computer. For example, two matrices may both have a determinant of $1.0e-8$, and yet one may be singular and the other may have a solution. In the first case, the difference between 0.0 and $1.0e-8$ is due to rounding error. One method for detecting the difference between such matrices is to scale them both by a large number (one consequence of the first property given for determinants is that any determinant can be made arbitrarily small or large by multiplying the matrix by the appropriate constant). If the matrix is singular, the new determinant will still be close to zero. If the matrix is nonsingular, the new determinant will be the old determinant times the scaling factor.

An overdetermined system of equations arises when two or more equations are inconsistent. For example, the system of equations

$$\begin{aligned} y &= 3 \\ y &= 2 \end{aligned} \qquad (7.13)$$

is overdetermined. There is no solution for y that satisfies both equations.

At first glance, it might seem that an overdetermined system can be identified easily by the fact that there are more equations than unknowns, resulting in a matrix that is not square. You cannot, however, assume that any system with a nonsquare matrix is overdetermined, for some of the equations may be linearly dependent. Such a system may be overdetermined, it may have a solution, or it may be underdetermined. How can you test a nonsquare matrix to determine whether it is a solution?

The presence of a nonzero determinant does not guarantee that a solution to the set of equations can be found. Some matrices are *ill-conditioned;* that is, they are sensitive to rounding errors in the arithmetic operations required to find the solution. There is no simple test that identifies an ill-conditioned matrix. Several of the references at the end of the chapter discuss algorithms that can be used to minimize the errors in matrix manipulation.

A general formula for the determinant

There are several equivalent formulas for calculating the determinant. None of the formulas has intuitive or physical interpretations, because the determinant is simply an arbitrary (but useful) combination of the elements of a matrix. This discussion will be limited to finding the determinant using the method of minors and cofactors.

The *minor M_{ij}* of matrix A is formed by deleting row i and column j from the matrix A. For example, the minor M_{11} of matrix A from Equation 7.7 is

$$\begin{bmatrix} 6 & -2 \\ -2 & 16 \end{bmatrix}$$

The *cofactor A_{ij}* is the determinant of the minor M_{ij} with the appropriate sign. The sign of the cofactor is determined by whether the sum of $i + j$ is odd or even:

$$A_{ij} = (-1)^{i+j} \det M_{ij} \tag{7.14}$$

Notice that the minor is a matrix and the cofactor is a scalar value.

The determinant of A can be found by expanding the cofactors of any row or column as shown by Equation 7.15. Expanding by cofactors is difficult to do by hand and is usually done with a computer. If the matrix is expanded by columns, the determinant of A is the sum of the elements of a column times its cofactor. If A is expanded by rows, the determinant of A is the sum of the elements of a row times its cofactor; that is,

$$\det A = \sum_{k=1}^{n} a_{ik} A_{ik} \tag{7.15}$$

Equation 7.15 expresses the determinant of the n by n matrix A in terms of determinants of minors that are $(n - 1)$ by $(n - 1)$ matrices. If A is, for example, a 20 by 20 matrix, its minors are 19 by 19 matrices. The determinant of each 19 by 19 minor must be found by expanding it in cofactors, whose minors are 18 by 18 matrices, and so on. When the minors have been reduced to 3 by 3 matrices, the value of the determinant can be found using Equation 7.9. An algorithm can be written to compute the determinant from Equation 7.15 using iteration, but the algorithm is simpler to write using recursion (see Chapter 15). In Problem 3, you are asked to compute the determinant from Equation 7.15 using a recursive function.

Solution to Case Study 7

Now that the notation for writing a system of simultaneous equations has been developed, the original algorithm for Case Study 7 for the solution of three simultaneous equations can be refined. One difference between the original algorithm and the refined algorithm is that a function for the determinant has been created.

ALGORITHM 7.2   Refinement of algorithm 7.1

begin algorithm
1. Read the coefficient matrix **Coeff** for the equations that have been derived from the voltages and resistances
2. Compute the determinant of the matrix **Coeff**
   DetCoeff ← Determinant3(Coeff)

3. Test the value of **DetCoeff**
     If **DetCoeff** $<> 0$ then
          write 'A solution for the circuit exists, and the solution is
              unique.'
     else
          write 'A unique solution for the circuit does not exist.'
end algorithm

Case Study 7 requires that only the coefficient matrix be stored; however, the case studies in the following sections will also require storage locations for the values of the right-hand side of the equations and the unknown currents. Therefore, a general data structure and input procedure will be developed now. A data structure for the simultaneous equations is

```
const MaxRows = 3;              (* maximum number of equations - *)
                                (* that is, rows in the matrix. *)
      MaxColumns = 3;           (* maximum number of variables - *)
                                (* that is, columns in the matrix. *)

type  Matrix = array [1..MaxRows, 1..MaxColumns] of real;
      ColumnVector = array [1..MaxColumns] of real;

var   Coeff : Matrix;           (* matrix of coefficients. *)
      RightHandSide : ColumnVector;  (* right hand side. *)
      Current : ColumnVector;   (* solutions for the circuit. *)
      NumEqus : integer;        (* number of equations in the *)
                                (* system. *)
```

In this data structure, the coefficients of the equations are stored in the array **Coeff,** the values for the right-hand side are stored in **RightHandSide,** and the values calculated for x are stored in **Current.** It is understood by convention that, for example, **Coeff [1,3]** is the coefficient of x_3, the third unknown variable in Equations 7.5.

The input procedure **ReadData** simply requests the data on the coefficients and the right-hand sides of the equations.

```
procedure ReadData (var NumEqu : integer; var CoeffMatrix : Matrix;
               var RHS : ColumnVector);
(*      This procedure reads the number of equations, the coefficients,    *)
(*      and the right-hand side of a system of three linear equations.     *)

var   EquNum : integer;     (* for statement control variable for the *)
                            (* equations. *)
      Col : integer;        (* for statement control variable for the *)
                            (* columns (variables). *)
```

```
begin
  writeln (' You will be prompted to enter the number of equations,');
  writeln (' the coefficients for each equation, and the right-hand',
          ' side of the equations');
  writeln;
  writeln (' How many equations are there in this system?');
  readln (NumEqu);
  while NumEqu > MaxRows do
    begin
      writeln (' The maximum number of equations is ', MaxRows:1,
              '.  Please re-enter.');
      readln (NumEqu)
    end;

  for EquNum := 1 to NumEqu do
    begin
      writeln (' For equation ', EquNum:1, ' enter the ', NumEqu:1,
              ' coefficients');
      for Col := 1 to NumEqu do
        read (CoeffMatrix [EquNum, Col]);
      readln;
      writeln (' Enter the value of the right-hand side');
      readln (RHS [EquNum])
    end
end; (* procedure ReadData *)
```

Program 7.1, **CheckSolution,** is a short program that reads the coefficients of the simultaneous equations into an array, computes the determinant, and prints a message stating whether a unique solution exists.

PROGRAM 7.1 CheckSolution

```
program CheckSolution (input, output);
(*      Program CheckSolution reads the coefficients of the matrix for a     *)
(*      system of simultaneous equations and determines whether they have    *)
(*      a solution.                                                          *)

const MaxRows = 3;                      (* maximum number of equations - *)
                                        (* that is, rows in the matrix. *)

      MaxColumns = 3;                   (* maximum number of variables - *)
                                        (* that is, columns in the matrix. *)

      Small = 1.e-06;                   (* if the determinant is less *)
                                        (* small, it is considered to be *)
                                        (* equal to zero. *)
```

```
type   Matrix = array [1..MaxRows, 1..MaxColumns] of real;
       ColumnVector = array [1..MaxColumns] of real;

var    Coeff : Matrix;                      (* equation coefficients. *)
       RightHandSide : ColumnVector;        (* right hand side of the equa- *)
                                            (* tions. *)
       Current : ColumnVector;              (* solutions for the circuit. *)
       Det : real;                          (* determinant of matrix Coeff. *)
       NumEqus : integer;                   (* number of equations in the *)
                                            (* system. *)

(*$i determinant3 *)
(*$i readdata *)


(*-------------------------------------------------------------------------*)
begin (* main *)
   writeln (' This program reads a system of equations from the terminal');
   writeln (' and computes the determinant to test if a solution exists.');
   writeln (' This program will work correctly only if the number of',
             ' equations is three');
   writeln;

   ReadData (NumEqus, Coeff, RightHandSide);

   if NumEqus = 3 then
     begin
       Det := Determinant3 (Coeff);

       if abs (Det) > Small then
         writeln (' A solution for the circuit exists, and the solution is',
                   ' unique')
       else
         writeln (' A unique solution for the circuit does not exist')
     end
end. (* program CheckSolution *)
```

```
=>
 This program reads a system of equations from the terminal
 and computes the determinant to test if a solution exists.
 This program will work correctly only if the number of equations is three

 You will be prompted to enter the number of equations,
 the coefficients for each equation, and the right-hand side of the equations
```

```
How many equations are there in this system?
□3
For equation 1 enter the 3 coefficients
□12.0  -4.0  -8.0
Enter the value of the right-hand side
□30.0
For equation 2 enter the 3 coefficients
□-4.0  6.0  -2.0
Enter the value of the right-hand side
□-24.0
For equation 3 enter the 3 coefficients
□-8.0  -2.0  16.0
Enter the value of the right-hand side
□0.0
A solution for the circuit exists, and the solution is unique
```

Problems

1. Which of the following systems of equations have solutions? To answer the question, set up the coefficient matrix and compute the determinant for each system of equations.

(a) $x + 3y = 2$
$\quad\;\; 2x - 5y = 1$

(b) $x \quad\;\; + z = 1$
$\quad\;\; 2x + y - z = 3$
$\quad\;\; 3x \quad\;\; + 3z = 5$

(c) $x + 2y - z = 0$
$\quad\;\; x \quad\;\; + 2z = -3$
$\quad\;\; 2x - y + 3z = 1$

(d) $x + 3y + 2z = 20$
$\quad\;\; 3x - 2y - z = 10$
$\quad\;\; -x + y + z = -5$

2. Write a program that reads two matrices and returns the determinant of each of the matrices, the determinant of the sum of the matrices, and the determinant of the product of the matrices. The program should check that the sum and product matrices exist before reporting the determinants.

3. Write a recursive function for computing the determinant using minors and cofactors. Test your function by computing the determinant of the matrix for Case Study 7.

Solving Simultaneous Equations

In this section, four different methods will be presented for solving simultaneous linear equations: hand calculation, Cramer's rule, Gaussian elimination, and matrix inversion.

Current flow in a three-loop circuit

In the previous section, the three-loop direct current (DC) circuit in Case Study 7 was described in matrix form using linear equations. The tests made on the determinant showed that the circuit has a unique solution for the current flowing in each loop. Write a program to compute the current that flows in each loop.

Algorithm development

The structure of the algorithm for Case Study 8 is similar to that of the algorithm for Case Study 7. In Case Study 8 you must solve for the current rather than compute the determinant. Algorithm 8.1 assumes that the equations for the circuit have been set up as they were in the previous section. The right-hand sides of the equations are needed to compute the current, so they are included in the input to the program.

ALGORITHM 8.1   Algorithm to find the current in a three-loop DC circuit

begin algorithm
  1. Read the **Coeff** matrix and the **RightHandSide**
  2. Solve for the **Current**
  3. Report the **Current**
end algorithm

Substitution of variables

Given the system of three equations and three unknowns that was developed in the previous section,

$$
\begin{aligned}
12x_1 - 4x_2 - 8x_3 &= 30 \\
-4x_1 + 6x_2 - 2x_3 &= -24 \\
-8x_1 - 2x_2 + 16x_3 &= 0
\end{aligned}
\tag{8.1}
$$

you can solve for the values of x_1, x_2, and x_3 by substitution. There are many different ways to perform the substitution. Our plan of attack will be to combine the first and second equations, eliminating x_1, to get x_2 in terms of x_3. Then the second and third equations will be combined, eliminating x_1 and yielding another equation for the relationship between x_2 and x_3.

The first equation can be written to give x_1 in terms of x_2 and x_3:

$$
x_1 = \frac{15 + 2x_2 + 4x_3}{6}
\tag{8.2}
$$

Substituting Equation 8.2 for x_1 in the second equation yields

$$
-4\left(\frac{15 + 2x_2 + 4x_3}{6}\right) + 6x_2 - 2x_3 = -24
$$

or
$$
\tag{8.3}
$$
$$
7x_2 - 7x_3 = -21
$$

The second equation of System 8.1 can be written to give x_1 in terms of x_2 and x_3 as follows:

$$
x_1 = \frac{-24 - 6x_2 + 2x_3}{-4}
\tag{8.4}
$$

Substituting Equation 8.4 for x_1 in the last equation of System 8.1 yields

$$
-7x_2 + 10x_3 = 24
\tag{8.5}
$$

The system of equations has been reduced to two equations (8.3 and 8.5) with two unknowns (x_2 and x_3). It is now easy to solve for x_2 and x_3. Continuing with the substitution method, solve Equation 8.5 for x_2:

$$
x_2 = \frac{10x_3 - 24}{7}
\tag{8.6}
$$

Finally, substituting Equation 8.6 for x_2 in Equation 8.3 yields a numerical value for x_3:

$$
x_3 = 1
\tag{8.7}
$$

Given the value for x_3, the values for x_2 can be found from Equation 8.6:

$$x_2 = -2 \tag{8.8}$$

Given the values for x_2 and x_3, any one of the original equations can be used to find the value of x_1. From Equation 8.2, the value of x_1 is

$$x_1 = \frac{5}{2} \tag{8.9}$$

You can verify that the values of x_1, x_2, and x_3 are correct by substituting the values into System 8.1:

$$12\left(-\frac{5}{2}\right) - 4(-2) - 8(1) = 30$$

$$-4\left(-\frac{5}{2}\right) + 6(-2) - 2(1) = -24$$

$$-8\left(-\frac{5}{2}\right) - 2(-2) + 16(1) = 0$$

As long as the DC circuit has only two or three loops, the hand substitution method is fairly easy to use, but if the number of equations is greater than three, this technique becomes unwieldy. An alternative is to use a technique that solves the problem in a general way and can be easily programmed on the computer. Two techniques will be covered for solving the simultaneous linear equations written in matrix form: Cramer's rule and Gaussian elimination.

Cramer's rule

Cramer's rule is a method for solving a given set of simultaneous equations using the determinant of the coefficient matrix. If you are solving simultaneous equations by hand, Cramer's rule is usually the best choice.

Cramer's rule states that the solution for the unknown variables x in the set of equations

$$Ax = b$$

is given by

$$x_j = \frac{\det B_j}{\det A} \quad \text{for } j = 1, \ldots, n \tag{8.10}$$

where n is the dimension of the matrix and B_j is the A matrix with column j replaced by the column vector b, or the right-hand side. For example,

$$B_3 = \begin{vmatrix} a_{11} & a_{12} & b_1 \\ a_{21} & a_{22} & b_2 \\ a_{31} & a_{32} & b_3 \end{vmatrix}$$

Algorithm 8.2 solves a system of simultaneous equations using a general formulation of Cramer's rule. The coefficients of the matrix are stored in the square 2 by 2 array **Coeff,** the right-hand side is stored in the array **RightHandSide,** and the solution is returned in the array **Solution.**

ALGORITHM 8.2   Algorithm for Cramer's rule

begin algorithm

1. Compute the determinant of the **Coeff** matrix
      DetCoeff ← Determinant(Coeff)

2. Compute the unknown vector **X**
      for **J** := 1 to **NumCols** do
         begin
            a. Create the **Bj** matrix
                  Replace column **J** of **Coeff** with **RightHandSide**
            b. Compute **Solution[J]**
                  Solution[J] ← Determinant(Bj) / DetCoeff
         end for
   end algorithm

Of the steps given in the algorithm above, Step 2a, which replaces columns in the **Coeff** matrix with the right-hand-side vector, is the only step that requires further refinement. In the algorithm for Step 2a, you should not lose the **Coeff** matrix in the process of creating the **Bj** matrices. Before replacing the columns in the **Coeff** matrix, you must first create a copy of the **Coeff** matrix and then replace the column by the right-hand side, as is done in the procedure **ReplaceColumn:**

```
procedure ReplaceColumn (N : integer; A : Matrix; RHS : ColumnVector;
                         ColumnNumber : integer; var B : Matrix);
(*      Procedure ReplaceColumn replaces ColumnNumber in the N by N      *)
(*      matrix A with the RHS (right-hand-side) vector.  The new matrix  *)
(*      is returned in the matrix B.                                     *)

var   Row : integer;       (* for statement control variable. *)

begin
   B := A;                 (* copy the A matrix into the B matrix. *)

   (* The statements below set the column numbered ColumnNumber in the B *)
   (* matrix to the column vector of the right-hand side.  The rest of the *)
   (* elements of B are unchanged. *)

   for Row := 1 to N do
      B [Row, ColumnNumber] := RHS [Row]
end; (* procedure ReplaceColumn *)
```

Given the procedure **ReplaceColumn** and the function **Determinant,** the main body for a procedure for Cramer's Rule can be written directly from the algorithm, with some changes in the identifiers in order to enhance the readability of the program.

```
procedure Cramers (N : integer; A : Matrix; RHS : ColumnVector;
                   var X : ColumnVector);
(*      This procedure uses Cramer's rule to compute the solution to    *)
(*      the system of equations represented by the N by N coefficient   *)
(*      matrix A and the right-hand-side vector RHS.  The solution is    *)
(*      returned in the vector X.                                        *)

var   BJ : Matrix;       (* the matrix A with column J replaced by the *)
                         (* right-hand-side column vector. *)
      DetA : real;       (* the determinant of matrix A. *)
      Col : integer;     (* for statement control variable. *)

(*$i replacecolumn *)
(*$i determinant3 *)

begin (* body of procedure Cramers *)
  DetA := Determinant3 (A);

  for Col := 1 to N do
    begin
      ReplaceColumn (N, A, RHS, Col, BJ);
      X [Col] := Determinant3 (BJ) / DetA
    end
end; (* procedure Cramers *)
```

First solution to Case Study 8

Once the procedure **Cramer** has been written, only the procedures **ReadData** and **ReportTheSolution** are needed to complete the program that solves the problem.

PROGRAM 8.1 CramersSolution

```
program CramersSolution (input, output);
(*      This program calls the procedure Cramer to solve a system of    *)
(*      equations.  This version of the program will work only for a     *)
(*      system of three equations.                                       *)

const MaxRows = 3;                    (* maximum number of equations - *)
                                      (* that is, rows in the matrix. *)
      MaxColumns = 3;                 (* maximum number of variables - *)
                                      (* that is, columns in the matrix. *)
```

```
type   Matrix = array [1..MaxRows, 1..MaxColumns] of real;
       ColumnVector = array [1..MaxColumns] of real;

var    Coeff : Matrix;                    (* equation coefficients. *)
       RightHandSide : ColumnVector;      (* right-hand-side of the equa- *)
                                          (* tions. *)
       Current : ColumnVector;            (* solutions for the circuit. *)
       NumEqus : integer;                 (* number of equations in the *)
                                          (* system. *)

(*$i cramers *)
(*$i readdata *)


(*$i reportthesolution *)
(*   procedure ReportTheSolution (N : integer; A : Matrix;              *)
(*                       RHS : ColumnVector; X : ColumnVector);    *)
(*         ReportTheSolution reports the solution to the equations      *)
(*         represented by the N by N matrix A and the right-hand-side   *)
(*         vector RHS.  The solution is stored in the vector X.         *)


(*------------------------------------------------------------------------*)
begin (* main program *)
  writeln (' This program computes the solution to a system of equations');
  writeln (' using Cramer''s rule.');
  writeln (' Unless the determinant function is modified, this program');
  writeln (' will work only for a system with three equations.');
  writeln;

  ReadData (NumEqus, Coeff, RightHandSide);

  Cramers (NumEqus, Coeff, RightHandSide, Current);

  ReportTheSolution (NumEqus, Coeff, RightHandSide, Current)
end. (* program CramersSolution *)


=>
 This program computes the solution to a system of equations
 using Cramer's rule.
 Unless the determinant function is modified, this program
 will work only for a system with three equations.

 You will be prompted to enter the number of equations,
 the coefficients for each equation, and the right-hand side of the equations
```

```
How many equations are there in this system?
□3
For equation 1 enter the 3 coefficients
□12.0  -4.0  -8.0
Enter the value of the right-hand side
□30.0
For equation 2 enter the 3 coefficients
□-4.0  6.0  -2.0
Enter the value of the right-hand side
□-24.0
For equation 3 enter the 3 coefficients
□-8.0  -2.0  16.0
Enter the value of the right-hand side
□0.0

For the set of equations

        12.00X1      -4.00X2      -8.00X3 =      30.00
        -4.00X1       6.00X2      -2.00X3 =     -24.00
        -8.00X1      -2.00X2      16.00X3 =       0.00

the values of X are

X1 =      2.50
X2 =     -2.00
X3 =      1.00
```

With Cramer's rule, you can solve the equations for the three-loop circuit quite quickly. If, however, there are more than three simultaneous equations, Cramer's rule becomes very inefficient because the general formula for the determinant must be used.

Gaussian elimination

Gaussian elimination is a general method for solving simultaneous equations based on the same methods that were used in the hand solution to the problem. In Gaussian elimination, the coefficient matrix and the constant vector are manipulated so that substituting and solving for variables can be performed easily at the end. Because Gaussian elimination involves many steps, the beginning of this section will cover the basic definitions and will give an overview of Gaussian elimination.

Upper-triangular form

The goal of the matrix manipulations in Gaussian elimination is to arrive at a matrix that is in *upper-triangular* form. In an upper-triangular matrix, all the elements below the main diagonal of the matrix are equal to 0. The remainder of the elements can have any value. Once the matrix is in upper-triangular form, the back substitution process described below is performed. The following 3 by 3 matrix is upper triangular:

$$\begin{bmatrix} a_{11} & a_{12} & a_{13} \\ 0 & a_{22} & a_{23} \\ 0 & 0 & a_{33} \end{bmatrix}$$

A special case of the upper-triangular matrix is the matrix with every element on the main diagonal equal to 1:

$$\begin{bmatrix} 1 & a_{12} & a_{13} \\ 0 & 1 & a_{23} \\ 0 & 0 & 1 \end{bmatrix}$$

Back substitution

When the matrix form of three simultaneous equations is

$$\begin{bmatrix} 1 & a_{12} & a_{13} \\ 0 & 1 & a_{23} \\ 0 & 0 & 1 \end{bmatrix} \quad \begin{bmatrix} x_1 \\ x_2 \\ x_3 \end{bmatrix} = \begin{bmatrix} b_1 \\ b_2 \\ b_3 \end{bmatrix}$$

the simultaneous equations are

$$\begin{aligned} x_1 + a_{12}x_2 + a_{13}x_3 &= b_1 \\ x_2 + a_{23}x_3 &= b_2 \\ x_3 &= b_3 \end{aligned} \tag{8.11}$$

Therefore, when the coefficient matrix is in upper-triangular form with 1s on the main diagonal, the value of x_3 is known. The equation represented by the last row in the matrix above is

$$x_3 = b_3 \tag{8.12}$$

and x_3 is immediately known to have a value of b_3.

The second row of the matrix represents the equation

$$x_2 + a_{23}x_3 = b_2 \tag{8.13}$$

Substituting the value of x_3 from Equation 8.12 in Equation 8.13 gives

$$x_2 = b_2 - a_{23}b_3 \tag{8.14}$$

The value of x_2 is now known, since b_3, b_2, and a_{23} are all known constants. This substitution process, called *back substitution,* is repeated until values for all the unknown variables have been determined.

Triangularization and normalization

Triangularization and normalization are the methods for obtaining a coefficient matrix in upper-triangular form so that the unknown variables can be found by back substitution. The problem is to find a way to get the correct matrix elements equal to 0 and 1.

The matrix A and the right-hand side b that represent the equations for the three-loop circuit in the case study are

$$A = \begin{bmatrix} 12 & -4 & -8 \\ -4 & 6 & -2 \\ -8 & -2 & 16 \end{bmatrix} \quad \text{and} \quad b = \begin{bmatrix} 30 \\ -24 \\ 0 \end{bmatrix}$$

To begin to work the matrix into the special upper-triangular form needed for back substitution, you can rewrite the equations so that element a_{11} is equal to 1.

The first row represents the equation

$$12x_1 - 4x_2 - 8x_3 = 30 \tag{8.15}$$

x_1 will have a coefficient of 1 if all the coefficients in Equation 8.15 are divided by 12:

$$x_1 - \frac{1}{3}x_2 - \frac{2}{3}x_3 = \frac{5}{2} \tag{8.16}$$

Because the equations are equivalent, Equation 8.15 can be replaced by Equation 8.16 in the system of simultaneous equations. The new coefficient matrix and the right-hand side are

$$\begin{bmatrix} 1 & -\frac{1}{3} & -\frac{2}{3} \\ -4 & 6 & -2 \\ -8 & -2 & 16 \end{bmatrix} \quad \begin{bmatrix} \frac{5}{2} \\ -24 \\ 0 \end{bmatrix}$$

The matrix now has a 1 as the first element of the main diagonal. Notice that the first element of the right-hand side has also changed.

The coefficient of any particular element is made equal to 1 by dividing all the elements of the row, including the right-hand side, by the coefficient that is to become 1. This process is called *normalization.* Since you know that the diagonal element is always the element set to 1, you can write a Pascal procedure to normalize a row of a matrix by its diagonal element.

```
procedure NormalizeRow (N : integer; var A : Matrix;
                    var RHS : ColumnVector; Row : integer);
(*      NormalizeRow divides the coefficients in a row of the square    *)
(*      matrix A by the diagonal element of that row.  The right-hand   *)
(*      side vector is also divided by the diagonal element of A.  The  *)
(*      resulting row of A has a 1.0 on the diagonal.  The new row      *)
(*      represents the same equation as the original row.               *)

var   Col : integer;          (* for statement control variable. *)
      Diagonal : real;        (* diagonal element of matrix A. *)

begin
  Diagonal := A [Row, Row];     (* save the original diagonal element. *)

  (* The following statements divide each element of the Row of the *)
  (* matrix A and the corresponding element of the right-hand side by *)
  (* the diagonal element of A.  *)

  for Col := 1 to N do
    A [Row, Col] := A [Row, Col] / Diagonal;
  RHS [Row] := RHS [Row] / Diagonal
end; (* procedure NormalizeRow *)
```

In order to triangularize a matrix, you must also be able to set an element in the matrix to 0 without changing the solution of the equations. To obtain a coefficient of 0 for an unknown variable in an equation, you must combine two equations. For example, to get a coefficient of 0 for x_1 in the second equation of the case study, look at the first two equations:

$$x_1 - \frac{1}{3}x_2 - \frac{2}{3}x_3 = \frac{5}{2} \tag{8.17}$$

and

$$-4x_1 + 6x_2 - 2x_3 = -24 \tag{8.18}$$

Multiplying the first equation by -4 and then subtracting it from the second equation yields

$$
\begin{aligned}
-4x_1 + 6x_2 - 2x_3 &= -24 \\
- -4x_1 + \frac{4}{3}x_2 + \frac{8}{3}x_3 &= -10 \\
\hline
0x_1 + \frac{14}{3}x_2 - \frac{14}{3}x_3 &= -14
\end{aligned} \tag{8.19}
$$

The resulting equation

$$\frac{14}{3}x_2 - \frac{14}{3}x_3 = -14 \tag{8.20}$$

can replace Equation 8.18 in the system of equations. The new coefficient matrix

$$\begin{bmatrix} 1 & -\frac{1}{3} & -\frac{2}{3} \\ 0 & \frac{14}{3} & -\frac{14}{3} \\ -8 & -2 & 16 \end{bmatrix} \quad \begin{bmatrix} \frac{5}{2} \\ -14 \\ 0 \end{bmatrix}$$

has the same solution as the original matrix.

To get a 0 as the coefficient of x_1 in the third row, use Equation 8.17,

$$x_1 - \frac{1}{3}x_2 - \frac{2}{3}x_3 = \frac{5}{2}$$

and the equation represented by the last row,

$$-8x_1 - 2x_2 + 16x_3 = 0 \qquad (8.21)$$

If Equation 8.21 is multiplied by -8 and subtracted from Equation 8.21, the coefficient of x_1 in the resulting equation is 0:

$$\begin{bmatrix} 1 & -\frac{1}{3} & -\frac{2}{3} \\ 0 & \frac{14}{3} & -\frac{14}{3} \\ 0 & -\frac{14}{3} & \frac{32}{3} \end{bmatrix} \quad \begin{bmatrix} \frac{5}{2} \\ -14 \\ 20 \end{bmatrix}$$

The algorithm to obtain a 0 coefficient for any particular element can be expressed as in Algorithm 8.3. The element **Coeff[TRow, TCol]**, which is to be set to 0, is called the *target element;* the row **TRow** is called the *target row;* and the column **TCol** is called the *target column.*

ALGORITHM 8.3   Algorithm to create a 0 coefficient a_{ij}

begin algorithm

   1. Create a row **K** with a 1 in column **TCol** using **NormalizeRow**

   2. Create a 0 in the target element
      for **Column** := 1 to **NumCols** do
        begin

          a. Multiply the current element by the target element
             Product ← **Coeff[K, Column]** * **Coeff[TRow, TCol]**
          b. Subtract this product from the corresponding element of
            the target row **TRow,** and replace the element in the
            target row by the result
             Coeff[TRow, Column] ← **Coeff[TRow, Column]** − **Product**
        end for
end algorithm

There are several points to be aware of in regard to Algorithm 8.3. For the algorithm to work, the equation to be multiplied by the appropriate coefficient and then subtracted from the target row must have a coefficient of 1 in the target column. Step 1 is therefore an important step. Another point to be aware of is that the target element **Coeff[TRow, TCol]** is in the target row that is replaced in Step 2. Depending on how the algorithm is implemented, the replacement may be made either after all the elements of the new row have been computed or as each new element is computed. If the replacement is made as each element is computed, you must be careful not to lose the original value of **Coeff[TRow, TCol].** The procedure below creates a 0 in the matrix element **Coeff[TRow, TCol]** using the second strategy, storing the value of the target element in a temporary variable **Temp.**

```
procedure CreateAZero (N : integer; var A : Matrix; var B : ColumnVector;
                       TRow, TCol, NormRow : integer);
(*      CreateAZero creates a zero in the target element A[TRow, TCol].      *)
(*      NormRow is the index of a row that has a one in column TCol.         *)
(*      The matrix A is a square N by N matrix.                             *)

var   Col : integer;              (* for statement control variable. *)
      TargetValue : real;         (* value  stored in the target *)
                                  (* element before the 0 is created. *)
begin
  TargetValue := A [TRow, TCol];      (* A [TRow, TCol] is the target *)
                                      (* element that becomes zero. *)

  (* The following statements go across the columns of row TRow subtract- *)
  (* ing the element at A [NormRow, Col] times the target element.  The *)
  (* effect of this operation is to subtract row NormRow from row TRow.  *)
  (* Because row TRow represents an equation, the same operation must be *)
  (* performed on its right-hand-side.  NormRow is the index of a norm- *)
  (* alized row that has a 1 in column TCol. *)

  for Col := 1 to N do
    A [TRow, Col] := A [TRow, Col] - A [NormRow, Col] * TargetValue;

  B [TRow] := B [TRow] - B [NormRow] * TargetValue
end; (* procedure CreateAZero *)
```

To see the importance of the temporary variable, substitute **Coeff[TRow, TCol]** for **Temp** in the fragment, then perform a walkthrough with **Coeff[2, 1]** as the target element. You will see that the value of **Coeff[TRow, TCol]** changes from -4 to 0 the first time through the **for** loop. When the loop executes the second time, the value of **Coeff[2, 2]** is set to $6 - \left(-\frac{1}{3}\right) * (0)$ instead of $6 - \left(-\frac{1}{3}\right) * (-4)$. All of the subsequent computations, including the computation for the right-hand side, will be incorrect.

Given the algorithms to normalize a row and create a 0 in a particular target element, the next step in the Gaussian elimination is to create a matrix with 0s below the diagonal and 1s on the diagonal. An algorithm for obtaining an upper-triangular matrix with 1s on the diagonal is given in Algorithm 8.4.

ALGORITHM 8.4 Algorithm to obtain an upper triangular matrix with 1s on diagonal

begin algorithm

  1. Starting from the first row, obtain a coefficient of 1 in the diagonal element of each row using **NormalizeRow**

  2. Create 0s in the columns beneath the diagonal element of the row using the procedure **CreateAZero**

  3. Continue this process for each row, starting with the diagonal element in each row, until the matrix is in upper-triangular form

end algorithm

After the first two steps of the algorithm have been executed for the first row, the matrix for the case study is

$$
\begin{bmatrix}
1 & -\frac{1}{3} & -\frac{2}{3} \\
0 & \frac{14}{3} & -\frac{14}{3} \\
0 & -\frac{14}{3} & \frac{32}{3}
\end{bmatrix}
\begin{bmatrix}
\frac{5}{2} \\
-14 \\
20
\end{bmatrix}
$$

After the algorithm has been repeated for each of the rows in the coefficient matrix, the final matrix in upper-triangular form is

$$
\begin{bmatrix}
1 & -\frac{1}{3} & -\frac{2}{3} \\
0 & 1 & -1 \\
0 & 0 & 1
\end{bmatrix}
\begin{bmatrix}
\frac{5}{2} \\
-3 \\
1
\end{bmatrix}
$$

You can test your understanding of Gaussian elimination and of the preceding algorithms by answering the following questions: Does the order in which the operations are performed affect the answer? Can the diagonal elements all be set to 1 at the beginning of the algorithm? Can the elements of the last row be computed first?

Alternative solution to Case Study 8

Once the matrix is in upper-triangular form, the values for the current in the circuit loops can be found using back substitution. The value for x_3 can be found from the last row of the matrix:

$$x_3 = 1$$

The equation for x_2 from the second row is

$$x_2 - x_3 = -3$$

Substituting the value 1 for x_3 results in

$$x_2 = -2$$

Taking the first row,

$$x_1 - \frac{1}{3}x_2 - \frac{2}{3}x_3 = \frac{5}{2}$$

and substituting the values for x_2 and x_3 yields

$$x_1 = \frac{5}{2}$$

In Problems 5 through 7, you are asked to complete the Gaussian elimination program. Completion of the program requires that you write a procedure to perform back substitution, finish the procedure to set the elements beneath the diagonal to 0, write input/output routines, and write the main program.

Matrix inversion

Matrix inverses can be used in the solution of many different types of problems, including those involving simultaneous equations. Another alternative to Case Study 8 will be presented using matrix inversion.

For the circuit case study, it would seem that there should be a way to solve for the values of the current x directly from the equation

$$Ax = b$$

If A were a number instead of a matrix, you could multiply the right-hand side by its reciprocal, $1/A$, to solve for x. The *inverse* of a matrix performs the same function as the *reciprocal* of a number. For numbers, the relationship

$$y\frac{1}{y} = 1$$

defines the reciprocal; for matrices, the relationship

$$AA^{-1} = I \tag{8.22}$$

defines the inverse. This section will develop an algorithm to solve for the matrix A^{-1} so that the vector x can be computed directly from the equation

$$x = A^{-1}b \tag{8.23}$$

Equation 8.22 states that the product of a matrix and its inverse is the identity matrix. The identity matrix, I in Equation 8.22, is the square matrix with 1s on the diagonal and 0s elsewhere. For example, the 5 by 5 identity matrix is

$$I = \begin{bmatrix} 1 & 0 & 0 & 0 & 0 \\ 0 & 1 & 0 & 0 & 0 \\ 0 & 0 & 1 & 0 & 0 \\ 0 & 0 & 0 & 1 & 0 \\ 0 & 0 & 0 & 0 & 1 \end{bmatrix}$$

For the case study, you are given the matrix A and you need to find its inverse. You know that the identity matrix will be the 3 by 3 matrix with 1s on the diagonal and 0s elsewhere. In Equation 8.22, the only unknown is the inverse of the matrix. To simplify the notation, call the unknown inverse C:

$$AC = I \tag{8.24}$$

A theorem from linear algebra states that the inverse of A, if it exists, is unique. Therefore, only one matrix C will satisfy Equation 8.24. The elements of C must be found such that multiplying matrix A by matrix C will result in 1s on the diagonal and 0s elsewhere:

$$\sum_{k=1}^{n} a_{ik} c_{kj} = \begin{cases} 1 & \text{if } i = j \\ 0 & \text{if } i \neq j \end{cases} \text{ for all } i, j \tag{8.25}$$

The elements c_{ij} that satisfy Equation 8.25 are the elements of the inverse matrix of A. Since the elements of the n by n matrix A are known, Equation 8.25 can be viewed as a system of n^2 equations with n^2 unknowns. The values for c_{ij} can be found using Gaussian elimination. This algorithm will give the inverse of the matrix, but it is not the most efficient method of finding the inverse since it requires that an n^2 by n^2 matrix be solved.

Another method for finding the inverse is based on the algorithms developed for Gaussian elimination that set particular elements of a matrix to 0s or 1s. The algorithm can be developed starting from Equation 8.26, which states that any matrix times the identity matrix equals itself:

$$AI = A \tag{8.26}$$

To avoid confusion later, the matrix I on the left-hand side of the equation will be renamed B:

$$AB = A$$

The rows of the matrix A on the right-hand side of Equation 8.26 can be manipulated so that 1s appear on the diagonal and 0s appear everywhere else. Each time an operation is performed on the matrix A, the same operation is performed on the matrix B. The matrix A will be transformed to the identity

matrix, while **B,** which was originally the identity matrix, is transformed to
A^{-1}. This algorithm is called *Gauss-Jordan elimination.*

A procedure to compute the inverse of a matrix requires two matrices:
one to store the matrix **A** as it is transformed into the identity matrix and one
to store the matrix **B** as it is transformed into A^{-1}. A third matrix to save the
original matrix **A** is not required, but should be included. Without the original
matrix, there is no way to test whether the inverse was computed correctly.
Also, for large matrices, it is sometimes necessary to modify the algorithm to
go back periodically to the original matrix in order to avoid accumulating
rounding errors.

Algorithm 8.5 sets out the steps to create a matrix inverse using
Gauss-Jordan elimination. In this algorithm, the following data structure is
used:

```
const MaxRows = 10;                 (* maximum number of rows in the *)
                                    (* matrix. *)
      MaxColumns = 10;              (* maximum number of columns in *)
                                    (* the matrix. *)

type  Matrix = array [1..MaxRows, 1..MaxColumns] of real;

var   Original : Matrix;            (* original coefficient matrix. *)
      Work : Matrix;                (* matrix to be transformed into *)
                                    (* the identity matrix. *)
      AInverse : Matrix;            (* matrix to be transformed into *)
                                    (* the inverse. *)
      NumRows, NumColumns : integer;  (* number of rows and columns in *)
                                    (* the Original matrix. *)
```

Original stores the original **A** matrix, **Work** is the **A** matrix that is transformed
to the identity matrix, and **AInverse** is the matrix that starts as the identity
matrix and is transformed to the inverse of **A.**

ALGORITHM 8.5   Algorithm to create a matrix inverse

begin algorithm

1. Create an identity matrix
   AInverse ← Identity
2. Transform the **Original** matrix to an identity matrix for each row
   I and column **J**
   a. Create a 1 on the diagonal of **Original**
      (i) Normalize the row **I** in **Original** by dividing all the
          elements in row **I** by the diagonal element **Original[I, I]**
      (ii) Divide all the elements in row **I** of matrix **AInverse** by
          Original[I, I]

    b. Create zeros in the off-diagonal elements of **Original**
       If **I** <> **J,** use the algorithm that was written for the
       Gaussian elimination to create a zero. Perform the same
       steps on both **Original** and **AInverse**
end algorithm

The algorithm to compute the inverse of the matrix is based on the
procedures **NormalizeRow** and **CreateAZero**, that were developed for the
Gaussian elimination program. The procedure **NormalizeRow** can be modified to normalize a row in the **Work** matrix and then to divide the
corresponding row in the **AInverse** matrix by the same factor:

```
procedure Normalize (N : integer; var D, DInverse : Matrix;
                     Row : integer);
(*     Normalize divides the coefficients in a row of the N by N     *)
(*     matrix D by its diagonal element.   It also divides the Row in  *)
(*     the DInverse matrix by the diagonal element of D.  This pro-   *)
(*     cedure uses the same algorithm as procedure NormalizeRow.      *)

var   Col : integer;          (* for statement control variable. *)
      Diagonal : real;        (* diagonal element of matrix D. *)

begin
  Diagonal := D [Row, Row];     (* save the original diagonal element *)

  for Col := 1 to N do
    begin
      D [Row, Col] := D [Row, Col] / Diagonal;
      DInverse [Row, Col] := DInverse [Row,Col] / Diagonal
    end
end; (* procedure Normalize *)
```

The procedure **SetZero** uses the algorithm that creates a 0 in a particular
row and column of the **Work** matrix. The procedure performs the same
operations on the **AInverse** matrix as on the **Work** matrix.

```
procedure SetZero (N : integer; var D, DInverse : Matrix;
                   RowNum, ColNum : integer );
(*     SetZero sets a zero in the element [RowNum, ColNum] of the N by  *)
(*     N matrix D.  Every operation performed on D is also performed    *)
(*     on the N by N matrix DInverse.                                   *)

var   Col : integer;          (* for statement control variable. *)
      TargetValue : real;     (* original value of the target element. *)
```

```
begin
  (* D [RowNum, ColNum] is the target element to become zero.  If it is *)
  (* already zero, this procedure does not have to be executed. *)

  if abs (D [RowNum, ColNum]) > 1.0e-06  then
    begin
      TargetValue := D [RowNum, ColNum];

      (* The following statements go across the columns of RowNum subtract- *)
      (* ing the element at D [ColNum, Col] times the target element.  The *)
      (* effect of this operation is to subtract the row ColNum from the *)
      (* row RowNum.  The same operation must be performed on DInverse.  *)

      for Col := 1 to N do
        begin
          D [RowNum, Col] := D [RowNum, Col] - D [ColNum, Col] * TargetValue;
          DInverse [RowNum, Col] :=  DInverse [RowNum, Col]
                                     - DInverse [ColNum, Col] * TargetValue
        end
    end  (* if  target not already zero *)
end; (* procedure SetZero *)
```

Finally, the **Normalize** and **SetZero** procedures can be included in a procedure that goes down the rows of each column of the **Work** matrix, setting the off-diagonal elements to zero until the **Work** matrix has been transformed into the **AInverse** matrix.

```
procedure Inverse (N : integer; A : Matrix; var AInverse : Matrix);
(*      Procedure Inverse inverts the N by N matrix, A, and returns        *)
(*      the inverse in the matrix AInverse.                                *)

var   Row, Column : integer;          (* for statement control variables. *)

(*$i normalize *)
(*$i setzero *)


  procedure CreateIdentity (M : integer; var B : Matrix);
  (*      CreateIdentity creates an identity matrix that is M by M.        *)

  var   Row, Col : integer;           (* for statement control variables. *)

  begin
    for Row := 1 to M do
      for Col := 1 to M do
        if Row <> Col then
          B [Row, Col] := 0.0         (* set off-diagonal elements to 0.0. *)
        else
          B [Row, Col] := 1.0         (* set diagonal elements to 1.0. *)
  end; (* procedure CreateIdentity *)
```

```
begin (* body of procedure Inverse *)

  CreateIdentity (N, AInverse);          (* create an identity matrix in *)
                                         (* AInverse. *)

  (* The following statements transform the matrix A to the identity *)
  (* matrix by creating ones on the diagonals and zeros on the off- *)
  (* diagonals.  As A is transformed to the identity matrix, AInverse *)
  (* is transformed to the inverse. *)

  for Column := 1 to N do
    for Row := 1 to N do
      begin
        Normalize (N, A, AInverse, Column);

        if Column <> Row then
          SetZero (N, A, AInverse, Row, Column)
      end  (* for Row *)
end; (* procedure Inverse *)
```

The procedure **Inverse,** as written, does not test for singular matrices or for division by zero. You are asked to develop several refinements to the procedure in Problem 10.

Checking the procedure **Inverse** requires a test program. One test of the procedure **Inverse** is to find the inverse of the identity matrix. If the procedure is working correctly the result will be the identity matrix, since the inverse of the identity matrix is the identity matrix. Another test is to multiply the original matrix by its computed inverse to ensure that the result is the identity matrix. Both of these tests are performed in Program 8.2, **TestInverse.**

PROGRAM 8.2   TestInverse

```
program TestInverse (input, output );
(*     This program tests the procedure Inverse by finding the inverse    *)
(*     of a matrix and then multiplying the inverse by the original       *)
(*     matrix.  The result should be the identity matrix.                 *)

const MaxRows = 10;              (* maximum number of rows in the matrix. *)

type  Matrix = array [1..MaxRows, 1..MaxRows] of real;

var   Original : Matrix;         (* original coefficient matrix. *)
      Work : Matrix;             (* matrix to be transformed into the identity *)
                                 (* matrix. *)
      AInverse : Matrix;         (* matrix to be transformed into the inverse. *)
      Result : Matrix;           (* the product of AInverse and Original. *)
      NumRows : integer;         (* number of rows in the matrix. *)
```

```
(*$i inverse *)

(*$i multiplymatrices *)
(*   procedure MultiplyMatrices (Num : integer; A, D : Matrix;           *)
(*                              var B : Matrix);                          *)
(*       Procedure MultiplyMatrices from Chapter 9 multiplies the Num     *)
(*       by Num matrices A and D and returns the result in B.             *)


(*$i inputdata *)
(*   procedure InputData (var N : integer; var AMatrix : matrix);         *)
(*       InputData reads the matrix coefficients from the terminal        *)
(*       and prints the initial message to the user.                      *)


(*$i echo *)
(*   procedure Echo (N : integer; AnyMatrix : Matrix);                    *)
(*       Echo prints the elements of AnyMatrix in matrix format.          *)


(*------------------------------------------------------------------------*)
begin (* main *)
  InputData (NumRows, Work);
  Original := Work;              (* save the original matrix. *)

  Inverse (NumRows, Work, AInverse);

  writeln;
  writeln (' Original Matrix');
  Echo (NumRows, Original);

  writeln;
  writeln (' Inverse Matrix');
  Echo (NumRows, AInverse);

  MultiplyMatrices (NumRows, Original, AInverse, Result);
  writeln;
  writeln (' The product of the original and inverse matrices is');
  Echo (NumRows, Result)
end. (* program TestInverse *)



=>
 This program reads a matrix, inverts it,
 and prints the product of the matrix and its inverse.
```

```
What is the dimension of the matrix?
□3
For row 1 enter the 3 coefficients
□1.0  0.0  0.0
For row 2 enter the 3 coefficients
□0.0  1.0  0.0
For row 3 enter the 3 coefficients
□0.0  0.0  1.0

Original Matrix
     1.00        0.00        0.00
     0.00        1.00        0.00
     0.00        0.00        1.00

Inverse Matrix
     1.00        0.00        0.00
     0.00        1.00        0.00
     0.00        0.00        1.00

The product of the original and inverse matrices is
     1.00        0.00        0.00
     0.00        1.00        0.00
     0.00        0.00        1.00

=>
This program reads a matrix, inverts it,
and prints the product of the matrix and its inverse.

What is the dimension of the matrix?
□4
For row 1 enter the 4 coefficients
□4.0  3.0  2.0  6.0
For row 2 enter the 4 coefficients
□9.0  6.0  -1.0  2.0
For row 3 enter the 4 coefficients
□4.0  8.0  76.0  1.0
For row 4 enter the 4 coefficients
□0.0  5.0  3.0  2.0

Original Matrix
     4.00        3.00        2.00        6.00
     9.00        6.00       -1.00        2.00
     4.00        8.00       76.00        1.00
     0.00        5.00        3.00        2.00

Inverse Matrix
     0.01        0.10        0.01       -0.14
    -0.08        0.04       -0.01        0.21
     0.01       -0.01        0.01       -0.01
     0.20       -0.09       -0.01       -0.01
```

```
The product of the original and inverse matrices is
    1.00      0.00      0.00      0.00
   -0.00      1.00      0.00      0.00
   -0.00      0.00      1.00      0.00
   -0.00      0.00     -0.00      1.00
```

The values of -0.00 in the product of **Original** and **AInverse** are due to rounding error.

Alternative solution to Case Study 8

The equations for the case study were written in the form

$$Ax = b \qquad (8.27)$$

If both sides of the equation are multiplied by A^{-1}, Equation 8.27 becomes

$$A^{-1}Ax = A^{-1}b$$

or   (8.28)

$$x = A^{-1}b$$

Equation 8.28 gives a solution for the values of the current that can be computed directly if A^{-1} is known.

Note that, because matrix multiplication is not commutative (in general, $AD \neq DA$), the order of the multiplication is important. Both sides of Equation 8.27 are multiplied by A^{-1} on the left. $A^{-1}b$ is not the same as bA^{-1}.

The completed procedure **Inverse** can be used in a program to compute the value of the currents in the simultaneous equations from the case study. The matrix A^{-1} can be multiplied by the right-hand-side vector b, and the resulting vector x is the solution to the set of simultaneous equations

$$x = A^{-1}b$$

Program 8.3 solves Case Study 8 using the matrix inverse.

PROGRAM 8.3 SolveByInverse

```
program SolveByInverse (input, output);
(*    Program SolveByInverse solves simultaneous equations using the    *)
(*    matrix inverse algorithm.                                         *)
```

```
const MaxRows = 10;                    (* maximum number of rows in the *)
                                       (* matrix. *)
      MaxColumns = 10;                 (* maximum number of columns in *)
                                       (* the matrix. *)

type  Matrix = array [1..MaxRows, 1..MaxColumns] of real;
      ColumnVector = array [1..MaxColumns] of real;

var   Coeff : Matrix;                  (* matrix of coefficients. *)
      RightHandSide : ColumnVector;    (* right-hand side of equations. *)
      Current : ColumnVector;          (* solutions for the circuit. *)
      CInverse : Matrix;               (* inverse of the Coeff matrix. *)
      NumRows : integer;               (* number of rows in the Coeff *)
                                       (* matrix. *)
      Col : integer;                   (* for statement control variable. *)

(*$i readdata *)
(*$i reportthesolution *)
(*$i inverse *)


  procedure Multiply (N : integer; A : Matrix; B : ColumnVector;
                    var Answer : ColumnVector);
  (*      Multiply multiplies a  matrix times the column vector and        *)
  (*      returns the result in the column vector Answer.                  *)

  var   Row, Col : integer;       (* for statement control variables. *)

  begin
    for Row := 1 to N do
      begin
        Answer [Row] := 0.0;

        for Col := 1 to N do
          Answer [Row] := Answer [Row] + A [Row, Col] * B [Col]
      end
  end; (* procedure Multiply *)



  (*-------------------------------------------------------------------*)

begin (* main *)
  ReadData (NumRows, Coeff, RightHandSide);
  Inverse (NumRows, Coeff, CInverse);
  Multiply (NumRows, CInverse, RightHandSide, Current);
  ReportTheSolution (NumRows, Coeff, RightHandSide, Current)
end. (* program SolveByInverse *)
```

```
=>
You will be prompted to enter the number of equations,
the coefficients for each equation, and the right-hand side of the equations

How many equations are there in this system?
□3
 For equation 1 enter the 3 coefficients
□12.0  -4.0  -8.0
 Enter the value of the right-hand side
□30.0
 For equation 2 enter the 3 coefficients
□-4.0  6.0  -2.0
 Enter the value of the right-hand side
□-24.0
 For equation 3 enter the 3 coefficients
□-8.0  -2.0  16.0
 Enter the value of the right-hand side
□0.0

 For the set of equations

        12.00X1      -4.00X2      -8.00X3 =      30.00
        -4.00X1       6.00X2      -2.00X3 =     -24.00
        -8.00X1      -2.00X2      16.00X3 =       0.00

 the values of X are

X1 =      2.50
X2 =     -2.00
X3 =      1.00
```

Problems

1. For those systems from Problem 1 for Application 7 that have solutions, compute the solutions by substitution of variables, by Cramer's rule, and by Gaussian elimination.

2. Compute the inverse of matrices A and B:

$$A = \begin{bmatrix} 1 & \frac{1}{2} \\ 2 & 1 \end{bmatrix} \qquad B = \begin{bmatrix} 1 & 3 \\ 2 & -5 \end{bmatrix}$$

3. In the set of linear equations

$$a_1 x + b_1 y = c_1$$
$$a_2 x + b_2 y = c_2$$

x and y are unknowns and the coefficients a_1, b_1, c_1, a_2, b_2, and c_2 are real numbers. Write a program that uses Cramer's rule to compute and report the solutions to the equations for the following two sets of values of the coefficients.

a_1	b_1	c_1	a_2	b_2	c_2
1.0	1.0	−1.0	−1.0	1.0	1.0
3.639	−5.502	8.216	−1.698	0.253	8.162

Within the program, verify that your solution is correct within an error of 1.0e−04.

4. Using Cramer's rule, write a program to solve the set of equations

$$\begin{aligned} x + y + z &= 2.2 \\ 2x - y + z &= 0.5 \\ x + 2y - z &= 1.9 \end{aligned}$$

and check the answer by substituting back into the equations. The program should write a report giving the value for each variable, the absolute value of the error for each variable, and the relative error for each variable. (See Chapter 5 in the main text.)

5. Write a procedure that transforms a square matrix into an upper-triangular matrix. Test your procedure by writing a main program that reads in a matrix, makes it upper triangular, and prints the new matrix. How can you test whether the upper-triangular matrix is equivalent to the original matrix? Can you include the test as part of the program?

6. Write a procedure that performs back substitution for a matrix in upper-triangular form. Test your procedure by writing a main program that reads in an upper-triangular matrix, solves for the unknown variables, and prints the results. How can you test whether the values for the unknown are correct? Can you include the test as part of the program?

7. Complete the Gaussian elimination program using the procedures from Problems 5 and 6. Test your program by solving the three-loop circuit case study from the chapter.

8. Make the Gaussian-elimination method for solving simultaneous equations more efficient and less prone to error in several ways:

   (a) Write a subprogram that tests whether any pair of equations is linearly dependent before the Gaussian elimination is started. Add your subprogram to the Gaussian elimination program. If a pair is linearly dependent, write a message to the user stating which pair is linearly dependent and exit from the program, since no unique solution exists.

   (b) *Sparse* matrices occur in many physical problems. A *sparce matrix* is a matrix with many zero elements. If the target element in the matrix is already zero, the elimination algorithm does not need to be performed for that element. Modify the upper-triangular procedure to test for a zero element before multiplying and subtracting.

(c) Write a procedure that rearranges the matrix so that the largest elements are on the diagonal. Having the largest elements on the diagonal reduces rounding errors and instabilities. The rearrangement can be physical (that is, the rows can be exchanged), or an array can be used to store the index of the rows in the rearranged order. For example, **RowIndex[1]** could contain the original row number of the first equation in the rearranged matrix. In the rest of the program, the index for the first row would be **RowIndex[1]. RowIndex** is called a *pointer* since it points to the rows in the proper order. Enter a matrix with very large and very small numbers. Run the Gaussian elimination program with and without invoking the rearrangement procedure. Are the answers the same?

9. Another method for solving simultaneous equations is the Gauss-Seidel method, which is an iterative method. In the Gauss-Seidel method, new values for variables are computed based on previous values, until the solution comes within a given tolerance. Given the system of equations

$$a_{11}x_1 + a_{12}x_2 + a_{13}x_3 = b_1$$
$$a_{21}x_1 + a_{22}x_2 + a_{23}x_3 = b_2$$
$$a_{31}x_1 + a_{32}x_2 + a_{33}x_3 = b_3$$

the values for each iteration are found using the following algorithm:

a. Guess an initial value for x_2 and x_3.
b. Using the values for x_2 and x_3, compute a value for x_1' using the equation

$$x_1' = \frac{b_1 - a_{12}x_2 - a_{13}x_3}{a_{11}}$$

This equation is just the first equation of the system rewritten to solve for x_1'. The values of x_1', x_2, and x_3 are the new solution values.
c. Use the value from Step b to compute a new value for x_2:

$$x_2' = \frac{b_2 - a_{21}x_1' - a_{23}x_3}{a_{22}}$$

Now the values of x_1', x_2', and x_3 are the current solution.
d. Use the solution from Step c to solve for a new value of x_3:

$$x_3' = \frac{b_3 - a_{31}x_1' - a_{33}x_2'}{a_{33}}$$

e. Compute the error in the most recent solution by substituting the values of x' for x in the equations and solving for b':

$$b_1' = a_{11}x_1' + a_{12}x_2' + a_{13}x_3'$$

If

$$|b_i' - b_i| < 10^{-6} \quad \text{for } i = 1, 2, 3$$

then stop. Otherwise, repeat the iteration process using the current values of x_1', x_2', and x_3', starting from Step b.

Write a program that solves a set of three simultaneous equations using the Gauss-Seidel method. Test your program by solving the circuit problem from Case Study 8.

10. Modify the matrix-inversion procedure to include the same refinements that were proposed for the Gaussian elimination algorithm in Problem 8.

11. For a physics experiment, you are studying the movement of a hockey puck on a smooth surface. You have taken 25 measurements of the velocity as a function of time. To find the relationship between velocity and time, you need to plot a straight line through the data points. Having plotted a straight line, you will know the initial velocity and the acceleration, since

$$v = v_0 + at$$

where a is the acceleration and v_0 is the initial velocity.

The most common method for selecting the best value is to use the *least-squares* criterion. This criterion minimizes the sum of the squares of the distances from each point to the straight line. If the line is given by

$$y = mx + b$$

where m is the slope and b is the intercept, the sum of the squared distances to the line is

$$E = \sum_{i=1}^{n} [y_i - (b + mx_i)]^2$$

where (x_i, y_i) are the paired observations and n is the number of observations. The error, E, is minimized when the following conditions are met:

$$nb + m \sum x_i = \sum y_i$$
$$b \sum x_i + m \sum x_i^2 = \sum x_i y_i$$

Notice that m and b are the unknowns in these equations. Since the x_i and y_i are all known, the sums in the above equations can be computed. The sums are the coefficients in the equations for the unknowns m and b. Use Gaussian elimination as a subprogram in a larger program that computes the least-squares line for up to 100 pairs of observations.

12. For Problem 11, suppose you have also taken 25 measurements of the distance traveled versus time. You want to find the least-squares curve for the distance versus time. This relationship is given by

$$x = v_0 t + \frac{1}{2}at^2$$

where x = the distance traveled

v_0 = the initial velocity

a = the acceleration

A straight line is not a good approximation to this curve. Instead, you need a quadratic:

$$y = mx^2 + bx + c$$

For a quadratic line, the error is minimized if the following three conditions are met:

$$nc + b \sum x_i + m \sum x_i^2 = \sum y^i$$
$$c \sum x_i + b \sum x_i^2 + m \sum x_i^3 = \sum x_i y_i$$
$$c \sum x_i^2 + b \sum x_i^3 + m \sum x_i^4 = \sum x_i^2 y_i$$

m, b, and c are the unknowns in these equations. Since the x_i and y_i are all known, the sums in the above equations can be computed. The sums are the coefficients in the equations for the unknowns m, b, and c. Use Gaussian elimination as a subprogram in a larger program that computes the least-squares quadratic line for up to 100 pairs of observations.

APPLICATION 9
Matrix Operations

CASE STUDY 9
Computer graphics

Translating, scaling, and rotating are three important functions of any computer graphics program. An object is *scaled* when it is stretched or compressed in either the *x*-direction or the *y*-direction or in both directions (Figure 9.1). An object is *translated* when it is moved along a linear path (Figure 9.2). An object is *rotated* when it is moved through an angle ϕ about the origin (Figure 9.3). Write a program that allows the user to specify a two-dimensional object and then to rotate, scale, or translate the object.

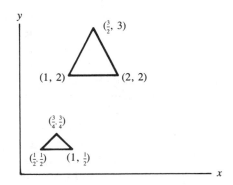

FIGURE 9.1
A triangle scaled by ½ in the *x*-direction and ¼ in the *y*-direction.

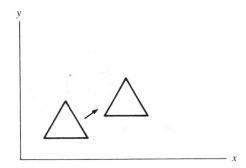

FIGURE 9.2
A triangle translated by the vector (1,1).

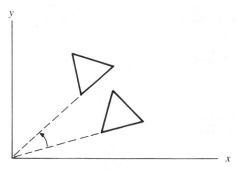

FIGURE 9.3
A triangle rotated about the
origin.

Algorithm development

For Case Study 9, there are two major problems to solve: how to store and manipulate an object within the computer and how to represent an object to the user. This section will focus on the first problem. Because Pascal does not have graphics capabilities, the second problem cannot be solved in a satisfactory manner with standard Pascal input/output.

Before writing the algorithm for the case study, you must decide how the object is to be represented in the computer. Each end point of an object can be thought of as a vector that represents the point's position in the *x-y* plane. The entire object can be changed by performing operations on the end points of the object. As long as the object is made up of straight lines, this strategy will work. In Chapter 9, procedures for scaling and adding individual vectors were developed. For the current problem, entire objects, rather than individual vectors, must be manipulated, and procedures for rotation will be required as well.

For Case Study 9, the coordinates of the object can be stored in a matrix in which each row corresponds to one point. With this strategy, the rectangle that is formed by connecting the points (1.0, 1.0), (2.0, 1.0), (2.0, 2.0), and (1.0, 2.0) can be represented by the matrix

$$P = \begin{bmatrix} 1.0 & 1.0 \\ 2.0 & 1.0 \\ 2.0 & 2.0 \\ 1.0 & 2.0 \end{bmatrix}$$

Notice that the end points do not specify a unique visual representation. The matrix above could represent either of the closed shapes in Figure 9.4.

FIGURE 9.4
Two figures represented by the matrix **P**.

This discussion is restricted to the internal representation of the object; its visual representation is ignored. In Chapter 16, a data structure using pointers is developed that allows you to specify which points are connected.

A Pascal data structure to store the end points of an object could consist of a data type for each end point and a data type for an object made up of end points, but because matrix operations will be used to manipulate the object, an array data structure is a better choice.

```
const MaxPoints = 25;            (* maximum number of end points *)
                                 (* allowed per object. *)
type  Coord = (XCoord, YCoord);  (* user-defined scalar for the x and y *)
                                 (* coordinates *)

      ObjectType = array [1..MaxPoints, Coord] of real;
```

Once the data structure has been decided on, the solution to the case study involves the development of algorithms to scale, translate, and rotate matrices. Algorithm 9.1 assumes that procedures will be developed to perform these matrix operations.

ALGORITHM 9.1   Algorithm for a graphics package

begin algorithm
    1. Initialize the program
       Read the end points of the **Object**
    2. Perform the matrix operations
       a. Ask the user what to do: rotate, scale, or translate
       b. Read **Answer**
       c. Select a procedure based on the user's choice
          case **Answer** of
             'r' : **Rotate(Object)**
             's' : **Scale(Object)**
             't' : **Translate(Object)**
          end
    3. Print the end points of the object
end algorithm

Additional input data will be needed for each of the procedures to be developed. For example, if **Rotation** is selected, the angle of rotation will be required. Because the information is different for each procedure, the specification for the additional input data will be included within the procedures.

Scaling a matrix

When an object is scaled, it is stretched or shrunk along the x- and y-axes by a constant. If a scaling constant is the same in the x and y directions, the scaling is said to be *uniform*. If the end points of the original object are specified by the matrix P and the scaling constant is s, the new end points of the uniformly scaled object can be found using scalar multiplication. The new matrix P' is given by

$$P' = sP \tag{9.1}$$

In *differential* scaling, the scale factors in the x and y directions do not have to be the same. For example, if the object represented by the matrix

$$\begin{bmatrix} x_1 & y_1 \\ x_2 & y_2 \\ x_3 & y_3 \end{bmatrix}$$

is scaled by s_x in the x direction and by s_y in the y direction, the new object is represented by the matrix

$$\begin{bmatrix} s_x x_1 & s_y y_1 \\ s_x x_2 & s_y y_2 \\ s_x x_3 & s_y y_3 \end{bmatrix}$$

To simplify, the coordinates of the new object are

$$x_1' = s_x x_1 \quad \text{and} \quad y_1' = s_y y_1 \tag{9.2}$$

and the matrix for the new object can be written as

$$\begin{bmatrix} x_1' & y_1' \\ x_2' & y_2' \\ x_3' & y_3' \end{bmatrix}$$

Representing differential scaling using scalar multiplication, as was done for uniform scaling in Equation 9.2, is difficult because the x- and y-coordinates must be multiplied by different factors. Differential scaling, however, can easily be represented using matrix multiplication as follows:

$$P' = PS$$

or

$$\begin{bmatrix} x_1' & y_1' \\ x_2' & y_2' \\ x_3' & y_3' \end{bmatrix} = \begin{bmatrix} x_1 & y_1 \\ x_2 & y_2 \\ x_3 & y_3 \end{bmatrix} \begin{bmatrix} s_x & 0 \\ 0 & s_y \end{bmatrix} \qquad (9.3)$$

Using the matrix multiplication formula from Chapter 9, you should be able to verify that x_1' in Equation 9.3 equals $s_x x_1$ as in Equation 9.2.

Procedure **ScaleMatrix** uses matrix multiplication to scale an object stored in an array of the type **ObjectType** by a scale factor of **ScaleX** in the x-direction and **ScaleY** in the y-direction.

```
procedure ScaleMatrix (N : integer; OldMat : ObjectType;
                       ScaleX, ScaleY : real; var NewMat : ObjectType);
(*      Procedure ScaleMatrix multiplies the coordinates of OldMat by      *)
(*      ScaleX in the x direction and ScaleY in the y direction to         *)
(*      create NewMat.                                                     *)

var   Point : integer;        (* for statement control variable. *)

begin
  for Point := 1 to N  do
    begin
      NewMat [Point, XCoord] := ScaleX * OldMat [Point, XCoord];
      NewMat [Point, YCoord] := ScaleY * OldMat [Point, YCoord]
    end
end; (* procedure ScaleMatrix *)
```

Translating a matrix

Translating an object requires that a translation vector (t_x, t_y) be specified that gives the change in the x-coordinate and the change in the y-coordinate. The translation vector is added to each of the end points of the object, as illustrated in Figure 9.5.

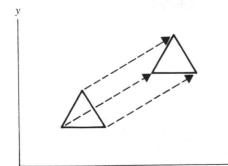

FIGURE 9.5
Translation of an object.

Through vector addition, an individual point can be translated by adding the translation vector to the vector from the origin to the point. Recall from Chapter 9 that vector addition is performed by adding the *x*-coordinates of each vector and the *y*-coordinates of each vector. Translating a matrix requires that the translation vector be added to each end point represented by a row in the matrix. The procedure **TranslateMatrix** simply adds the vector, with coordinates **TranslateX** and **TranslateY** in the parameter list, to each row of the matrix. The procedure **TranslateMatrix** uses the same data structures as **ScaleMatrix.**

```
procedure TranslateMatrix (N : integer; OldMat : ObjectType;
                           TransX, TransY : real; var NewMat : ObjectType);
(*      Procedure TranslateMatrix translates the matrix stored in OldMat    *)
(*      by a distance TransX in the x direction and TransY in the y         *)
(*      direction.  The translated matrix is returned in NewMat.            *)

var   Point : integer;      (* for statement control variable. *)

begin
  for Point := 1 to N  do
    begin
      NewMat [Point, XCoord] := TransX + OldMat [Point, XCoord];
      NewMat [Point, YCoord] := TransY + OldMat [Point, YCoord]
    end
end; (* procedure TranslateMatrix *)
```

An alternative method for translating an object will be discussed after matrix rotation has been covered.

Matrix rotation

Figure 9.6 illustrates a vector rotated through an angle ϕ. The magnitude of the vector remains constant as the angle changes. In Figure 9.6, the new values for θ', x', and y' are labeled.

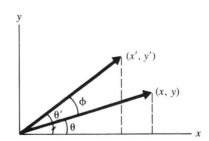

FIGURE 9.6
Rotation of a vector through an angle ϕ.

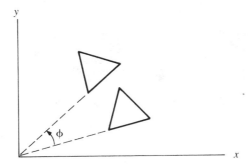

FIGURE 9.7
An object rotated through an angle ϕ about the origin.

Figure 9.7 illustrates rotation of an object through an angle ϕ by rotating each end point through the angle ϕ. In Figure 9.7, the object is rotated about the origin. Later we will develop an algorithm to rotate the object about its own center.

From Figure 9.6, you can see that it would be easier to express rotation in terms of the polar coordinates r and θ, rather than the Cartesian coordinates x and y. The values of r' and θ' are given by

$$r' = r$$

and   (9.4)

$$\theta' = \theta + \phi$$

But if a procedure to rotate a point specified by its polar coordinates were integrated into a graphics program that also used the procedures **ScaleMatrix** and **TranslateMatrix,** procedures to convert between polar and rectangular coordinates would be required. In the long run it is easier to specify the point to be rotated in rectangular coordinates. Looking at Figure 9.6, you can see that you can use trigonometric relationships to write the following equations for the coordinates of the point (x', y') in terms of the original point (x, y) and the rotation angle ϕ:

$$x' = x \cos \phi - y \sin \phi$$
$$y' = x \sin \phi + y \cos \phi$$ (9.5)

Equation 9.5 can be written in a compact form using matrix multiplication through the following transformation. If the matrix R is defined to be

$$R = \begin{bmatrix} \cos \phi & \sin \phi \\ -\sin \phi & \cos \phi \end{bmatrix}$$ (9.6)

and if the matrix P, representing the end points of the object, is multiplied by matrix R, the resulting matrix P' has the elements given in Equation 9.5. That is, if

$$P' = PR$$

or

$$\begin{bmatrix} x_1' & y_1' \\ x_2' & y_2' \\ x_3' & y_3' \end{bmatrix} = \begin{bmatrix} x_1 & y_1 \\ x_2 & y_2 \\ x_3 & y_3 \end{bmatrix} \begin{bmatrix} \cos \phi & \sin \phi \\ -\sin \phi & \cos \phi \end{bmatrix}$$

(9.7)

the resulting matrix P' has the elements

$$x_1' = x_1 \cos \phi - y_1 \sin \phi$$
$$y_1' = x_1 \sin \phi + y_1 \cos \phi$$

and so on.

The procedure **RotateMatrix** rotates an object specified by its Cartesian coordinates, again using the same data structure as the other procedures.

```
procedure RotateMatrix (N : integer; OldMat : ObjectType; Angle : real;
                        var NewMat : ObjectType);
(*      Procedure RotateMatrix rotates the matrix stored in OldMat      *)
(*      through the angle stored in Angle.  The coordinates of OldMat   *)
(*      are in rectangular coordinates.  The rotated matrix is returned *)
(*      in NewMat.                                                      *)

var   Point : integer;        (* for statement control variable. *)

begin
  for Point := 1 to N do
    begin
      NewMat [Point, XCoord] := OldMat [Point, XCoord] * cos(Angle)
                                - OldMat [Point, YCoord] * sin(Angle);
      NewMat [Point, YCoord] := OldMat [Point, XCoord] * sin(Angle)
                                + OldMat [Point, YCoord] * cos(Angle)
    end
end; (* procedure RotateMatrix *)
```

Refinements

An object scaled using Equation 9.3 is scaled about the origin rather than about the center of the object. Scaling a triangle about the origin by a factor of one-half produces the results illustrated in Figure 9.8(a). Figure 9.8(b) illustrates scaling a triangle by a factor of one-half about its own center.

Think about how a graphics program should operate from the user's point of view. Normally you would expect an object to be scaled about its center, an edge, or a vertex rather than the origin. The easiest way to scale an object about a point other than the origin is to translate the scaling point to the origin, perform the scaling, and then translate the point back to its original

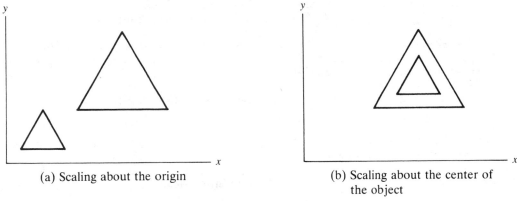

(a) Scaling about the origin

(b) Scaling about the center of
the object

FIGURE 9.8
Scaling an object.

location, as illustrated in Figure 9.9. The **ScaleMatrix** procedure can be
modified to include the point about which the object should be scaled in the
parameter list. **ScaleMatrix** invokes the procedure **TranslateMatrix** to translate the point to the origin. Notice that writing the **ScaleMatrix** procedure is
simplified by the fact that **TranslateMatrix**, which was developed as a separate
module, can be included and used in the procedure with no modifications.

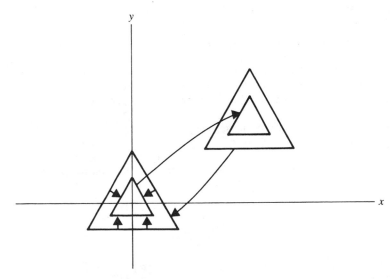

FIGURE 9.9
Scaling about the center of an object by translating the center to the origin, scaling,
then translating the center back to its original location.

```
procedure ScaleMatrix2 (N : integer; OldMat : ObjectType;
                        ScaleX, ScaleY : real; CenterX, CenterY : real;
                        var NewMat : ObjectType);
(*      The modified version of ScaleMatrix scales the OldMat about the    *)
(*      point (CenterX, CenterY) by translating the object to the origin,  *)
(*      then scaling, then translating the object back.                    *)

var   Point : integer;        (* for statement control variable. *)

begin
  (* Translate the center of the object to the origin by translating all *)
  (* the end points by (-CenterX, -CenterY). *)

  TranslateMatrix (N, OldMat, -CenterX, -CenterY, NewMat);

  for Point := 1 to N do
    begin
      NewMat [Point, XCoord] := ScaleX * OldMat [Point, XCoord];
      NewMat [Point, YCoord] := ScaleY * OldMat [Point, YCoord]
    end;

  (* Return the scaled object, stored in NewMat, to its original position *)
  (* by translating the center back to its original coordinates. *)

  TranslateMatrix (N, NewMat, CenterX, CenterY, NewMat)
end; (* procedure ScaleMatrix2 *)
```

Through the same modifications that were made to **ScaleMatrix,** the procedure **RotateMatrix,** which rotates the object about the origin, can be changed so that the center of rotation can be specified.

```
procedure RotateMatrix2 (N : integer; OldMat : ObjectType; Angle : real;
                         CenterX, CenterY : real; var NewMat : ObjectType);
(*      The modified version of RotateMatrix rotates the OldMat about      *)
(*      the point (CenterX, CenterY) by translating the object to the      *)
(*      origin, then rotating, then translating the object back.           *)

var   Point : integer;        (* for statement control variable. *)

begin
  (* Translate the center of the object to the origin by translating all *)
  (* the end points by (-CenterX, -CenterY). *)

  TranslateMatrix (N, OldMat, -CenterX, -CenterY, NewMat);

  for Point := 1 to N do
    begin
      NewMat [Point, XCoord] := OldMat [Point, XCoord] * cos(Angle)
                               - OldMat [Point, YCoord] * sin(Angle);
      NewMat [Point, YCoord] := OldMat [Point, XCoord] * sin(Angle)
                               + OldMat [Point, YCoord] * cos(Angle)
    end;
```

```
(* Return the scaled object, stored in NewMat, to its original position *)
(* by translating the center back to its original coordinates. *)

 TranslateMatrix (N, NewMat, CenterX, CenterY, NewMat)
end; (* procedure RotateMatrix2 *)
```

If an object is to be both scaled and rotated about the same point, the operations can be performed either individually or in a single step. If they are performed individually, the object is translated to the origin twice and back to its original location twice. Fewer operations are required if the object is translated to the origin, then scaled and rotated, then translated back to its original position. When performing both operations at once the *composition* of the scaling and rotation matrices may be computed using matrix multiplication:

$$C = SR \qquad (9.8)$$

where S = the scaling matrix (see equation 9.3)

R = the rotation matrix (see equation 9.6)

C = the composition matrix

Multiplying the end points of the object by C is equivalent to first multiplying the end points by S and then multiplying them by R. Therefore, multiplying by the new matrix, C, yields the new end points of the scaled and rotated object.

Translation is performed using matrix addition, but scaling and rotating are performed using matrix multiplication. If translation could be expressed in terms of matrix multiplication, the operations required to scale and rotate a matrix about a point other than the origin could be written in the compact form

$$C = T_1 R S T_2 \qquad (9.9)$$

where T_1 = the translation matrix that moves the point to the origin

R = the rotation matrix

S = the scaling matrix

T_2 = the matrix that translates the point back to its original position

Translation, scaling, and rotation can all be performed using matrix multiplication by adding an extra dimension to each point and to each matrix. The matrix P, representing the end points of the object in the new system, is

$$P = \begin{bmatrix} x_1 & y_1 & 1 \\ x_2 & y_2 & 1 \\ x_3 & y_3 & 1 \end{bmatrix} \qquad (9.10)$$

The first two elements that describe a point are the x- and y-coordinates, and the last element is always 1.

In the new coordinate system, an object can be translated by multiplying it by the translation matrix, which is defined as

$$T = \begin{bmatrix} 1 & 0 & 0 \\ 0 & 1 & 0 \\ t_x & t_y & 1 \end{bmatrix} \tag{9.11}$$

where t_x and t_y are the distances that the object is to be translated in the x and y directions, respectively. The translated matrix P' can now be found using matrix multiplication:

$$P' = PT$$

or

$$\begin{bmatrix} x_1' & y_1' & 1 \\ x_2' & y_2' & 1 \\ x_3' & y_3' & 1 \end{bmatrix} = \begin{bmatrix} x_1 & y_1 & 1 \\ x_2 & y_2 & 1 \\ x_3 & y_3 & 1 \end{bmatrix} \begin{bmatrix} 1 & 0 & 0 \\ 0 & 1 & 0 \\ t_x & t_y & 1 \end{bmatrix} \tag{9.12}$$

You can verify that multiplying the point $[x, y, 1]$ by the matrix T results in the translated point $[x + t_x, y + t_y, 1]$.

In the new coordinate system, the scaling matrix S is

$$S = \begin{bmatrix} s_x & 0 & 0 \\ 0 & s_y & 0 \\ 0 & 0 & 1 \end{bmatrix} \tag{9.13}$$

The new coordinates for a scaled point are

$$P' = PS$$

or

$$\begin{bmatrix} x_1' & y_1' & 1 \\ x_2' & y_2' & 1 \\ x_3' & y_3' & 1 \end{bmatrix} = \begin{bmatrix} x_1 & y_1 & 1 \\ x_2 & y_2 & 1 \\ x_3 & y_3 & 1 \end{bmatrix} \begin{bmatrix} s_x & 0 & 0 \\ 0 & s_y & 0 \\ 0 & 0 & 1 \end{bmatrix} \tag{9.14}$$

You can perform the matrix multiplication in Equation 9.14 to compute the values for x' and y' and to verify that they are consistent with Equation 9.2.

In the new system, the rotation matrix R is

$$R = \begin{bmatrix} \cos \phi & \sin \phi & 0 \\ -\sin \phi & \cos \phi & 0 \\ 0 & 0 & 1 \end{bmatrix} \tag{9.15}$$

The new coordinates for the rotated point are

$$P' = PR$$

or

$$\begin{bmatrix} x_1' & y_1' & 1 \\ x_2' & y_2' & 1 \\ x_3' & y_3' & 1 \end{bmatrix} = \begin{bmatrix} x_1 & y_1 & 1 \\ x_2 & y_2 & 1 \\ x_3 & y_3 & 1 \end{bmatrix} \begin{bmatrix} \cos \phi & \sin \phi & 0 \\ -\sin \phi & \cos \phi & 0 \\ 0 & 0 & 1 \end{bmatrix} \tag{9.16}$$

Again, you should be able to verify that Equation 9.16 is equivalent to Equation 9.5.

Solution to Case Study 9

Program 9.1 is the completed program for scaling, translating, and rotating the end points of an object.

PROGRAM 9.1 SimpleGraphics

```
program SimpleGraphics (input, output);
(*      This program can scale, rotate, and translate the end points of      *)
(*      an object.                                                           *)

const MaxPoints = 25;                   (* maximum number of end points *)
                                        (* allowed per object. *)
type  Coord = (XCoord, YCoord);         (* user-defined scalar for the x and y *)
                                        (* coordinates *)

      ObjectType = array [1..MaxPoints, Coord] of real;

var   NumPoints : integer;              (* number of points for the object. *)
      Object : ObjectType;              (* matrix of object end points. *)
      NewObject : ObjectType;           (* object after the operation has been *)
                                        (* performed. *)
      Operation : char;                 (* operation requested by the user. *)
      MoveX, MoveY : real;              (* distances by which the object is *)
                                        (* translated in the x and y *)
                                        (* directions. *)
      ChangeX, ChangeY : real;          (* scale factors in the x and y *)
                                        (* directions. *)
      AboutX, AboutY : real;            (* coordinates of the point about *)
                                        (* which the object will be scaled *)
                                        (* or rotated. *)
      Theta : real;                     (* angle through which the object is *)
                                        (* rotated. *)
(*$i translatematrix *)
(*$i scalematrix2 *)
(*$i rotatematrix2 *)
(*$i yesentered *)

  procedure ReadObject (var N : integer; var EndPoints : ObjectType);
  (*      ReadObject reads the number of end points and the coordinates      *)
  (*      of each end point for an object.                                   *)

  var Point : integer;        (* for statement control variable. *)

  begin
    writeln (' How many end points does the object have?');
    readln (N);
```

```
    while N > MaxPoints do
      begin
        writeln (' The maximum number of end points is', MaxPoints:1,
                 '.  Please re-enter.');
        readln (N)
      end;

    for Point := 1 to N do
      begin
        writeln (' Enter the X and Y coordinates of point ', Point:1);
        readln (EndPoints [Point, XCoord], EndPoints [Point, YCoord])
      end
end; (* procedure ReadObject *)

procedure ReadTranslateParameters (var TransX, TransY : real);
(*      This procedure reads the translation parameters from the user.     *)

begin
  writeln (' How far is the object translated in the x direction?');
  readln (TransX);
  writeln (' How far is the object translated in the y direction?');
  readln (TransY)
end; (* procedure ReadTranslateParameters *)


procedure ReadScaleParameters (var ScaleX, ScaleY,
                                   CenterX, CenterY : real);
(*      This procedure reads the scale parameters from the user.          *)

begin
  writeln (' What is the scale factor for the object in the x dimension?');
  readln (ScaleX);
  writeln (' What is the scale factor for the object in the y dimension?');
  readln (ScaleY);

  writeln (' Enter the x and y coordinates for the point about which the',
           ' object is scaled.');
  readln (CenterX, CenterY)
end; (* ReadScaleParameters *)


procedure ReadRotateParameters (var Angle, CenterX, CenterY : real);
(*      This procedure reads the rotation parameters from the user.       *)

begin
  writeln (' Through what angle is the point rotated?  Enter in radians.');
  readln (Angle);

  writeln (' Enter the x and y coordinates for the point about which the',
           ' object rotates.');
  readln (CenterX, CenterY)
end; (* ReadRotateParameters *)
```

```
procedure PrintObject (N : integer; Oper : char;
                       OldEndPoints, NewEndPoints : ObjectType);
(*      This procedure prints the end points of the operation after     *)
(*      operation has been performed.                                    *)

var Index : integer;        (* for statement control variable. *)

begin
  writeln;
  writeln (' The original endpoints were');
  writeln;
  writeln ('     X       Y');
  for Index := 1 to N do
     writeln (OldEndPoints [Index, XCoord]:6:1,
              OldEndPoints [Index, YCoord]:6:1);
  writeln;
  write (' After');
  case Oper of
    't', 'T' : write (' translating,');
    's', 'S' : write (' scaling,');
    'r', 'R' : write (' rotating,')
  end; (* case *)
  writeln (' the new endpoints are');
  writeln;
  writeln ('     X       Y');
  for Index := 1 to N do
     writeln (NewEndPoints [Index, XCoord]:6:1,
              NewEndPoints [Index, YCoord]:6:1)
end;   (* procedure PrintObject *)

procedure ReadOperation (var Oper : char);
(*      This procedure reads the operation requested by the user.        *)

begin
  repeat
    writeln;
    writeln (' What operation would you like to perform on the object?');
    writeln (' Enter');
    writeln ('      t    to translate the object');
    writeln ('      s    to scale the object');
    writeln ('      r    to rotate the object');
    writeln ('      e    to exit from the program.');

    readln (Oper)
  until Oper in ['t', 'T', 's', 'S', 'r', 'R', 'e', 'E']
end; (* procedure ReadOperation *)
```

```
(*--------------------------------------------------------------*)
begin
  ReadObject (NumPoints, Object);

  ReadOperation (Operation);

  while not (Operation in ['e', 'E']) do
    begin
      case Operation of
        't', 'T' : begin
                     ReadTranslateParameters (MoveX, MoveY);
                     TranslateMatrix (NumPoints, Object, MoveX, MoveY,
                                          NewObject)
                   end;
        's', 'S' : begin
                     ReadScaleParameters (ChangeX, ChangeY, AboutX, AboutY);
                     ScaleMatrix2 (NumPoints, Object, ChangeX, ChangeY,
                                      AboutX, AboutY, NewObject)
                   end;
        'r', 'R' : begin
                     ReadRotateParameters (Theta, AboutX, AboutY);
                     RotateMatrix2 (NumPoints, Object, Theta, AboutX, AboutY,
                                       NewObject)
                   end
      end; (* case *)

      PrintObject (NumPoints, Operation, Object, NewObject);

      ReadOperation (Operation);
      if not (Operation in ['e', 'E']) then
        begin
          writeln (' Do you want to use the new object?');
          if YesEntered then
            Object := NewObject
        end
    end (* while *)
end. (* program SimpleGraphics *)

=>
 How many end points does the object have?
 □3
 Enter the X and Y coordinates of point 1
 □0.0  0.0
 Enter the X and Y coordinates of point 2
 □2.0  0.0
 Enter the X and Y coordinates of point 3
 □1.0  1.0
```

```
What operation would you like to perform on the object?
Enter
      t    to translate the object
      s    to scale the object
      r    to rotate the object
      e    to exit from the program.
□t
 How far is the object translated in the x direction?
□1.0
 How far is the object translated in the y direction?
□1.0

 The original endpoints were

     X      Y
    0.0    0.0
    2.0    0.0
    1.0    1.0

 After translating, the new endpoints are

     X      Y
    1.0    1.0
    3.0    1.0
    2.0    2.0

 What operation would you like to perform on the object?
Enter
      t    to translate the object
      s    to scale the object
      r    to rotate the object
      e    to exit from the program.
□s
 Do you want to use the new object?
 Enter yes or no (y/n)
□y
 What is the scale factor for the object in the x dimension?
□0.5
 What is the scale factor for the object in the y dimension?
□0.5
 Enter the x and y coordinates for the point about which the object is scaled.
□0.0  0.0

 The original endpoints were

     X      Y
    1.0    1.0
    3.0    1.0
    2.0    2.0
```

After scaling, the new endpoints are

```
    X      Y
   0.5    0.5
   1.5    0.5
   1.0    1.0
```

What operation would you like to perform on the object?
Enter
        t   to translate the object
        s   to scale the object
        r   to rotate the object
        e   to exit from the program.
□r
 Do you want to use the new object?
 Enter yes ot no (y/n)
□y
 Through what angle is the point rotated? Enter in radians.
□1.0
 Enter the x and y coordinates for the point about which the object rotates.
□1.0 1.0

 The original endpoints were

```
    X      Y
   0.5    0.5
   1.5    0.5
   1.0    1.0
```

After rotating, the new endpoints are

```
    X      Y
   0.8    1.7
   1.4    2.5
   0.7    2.4
```

What operation would you like to perform on the object?
 Enter
        t   to translate the object
        s   to scale the object
        r   to rotate the object
        e   to exit from the program.
□e

Problems

1. Expand Program 9.1, **SimpleGraphics,** to plot the end points of the objects.

2. Program 9.1, **SimpleGraphics,** operates only on two-dimensional points. A three-dimensional point can be expressed in terms of its x-, y-, and z-coordinates, where the z-axis is perpendicular to the x- and y-axes:

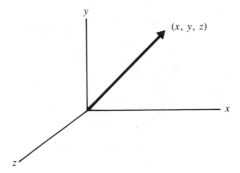

   The formulas to translate and scale points can easily be extended to three dimensions, but to rotate in three dimensions it is necessary to know which axis is the center of rotation. If the rotation in the two-dimensional model were duplicated in the three-dimensional model, the objects would be rotated about the z-axis:

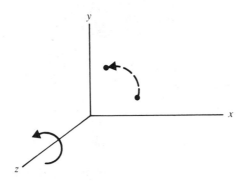

When an object is rotated around the x-axis,

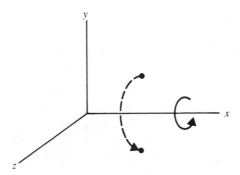

the new coordinates are given by

$$[x', y', x'] = [x, y, z] \begin{bmatrix} 1 & 0 & 0 \\ 0 & \cos\phi & \sin\phi \\ 0 & -\sin\phi & \cos\phi \end{bmatrix}$$

or

$$x' = x$$
$$y' = y \cos\phi - z \sin\phi$$
$$z' = y \sin\phi + z \cos\phi$$

When an object is rotated about the y-axis,

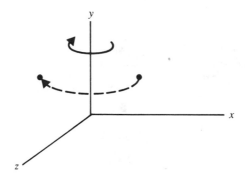

the new coordinates are given by

$$[x', y', x'] = [x, y, z] \begin{bmatrix} \cos\phi & 0 & -\sin\phi \\ 0 & 1 & 0 \\ \sin\phi & 0 & \cos\phi \end{bmatrix}$$

or

$$x' = x \cos\phi + z \sin\phi$$
$$y' = y$$
$$z' = -x \sin\phi + z \cos\phi$$

Write a program that rotates an object about the x-, y-, or z-axis at the request of the user.

3. The composition matrix for translating and scaling a matrix about a point,

$$C = T_1RST_2$$

can be extended to three-dimensional points. Translating can be expressed as matrix multiplication by adding another dimension to each point. The coordinates for a point in the new system are

$$[x, y, z, 1]$$

In the new coordinate system, the scaling matrix is

$$S = \begin{bmatrix} s_x & 0 & 0 & 0 \\ 0 & s_y & 0 & 0 \\ 0 & 0 & s_z & 0 \\ 0 & 0 & 0 & 1 \end{bmatrix}$$

The translation matrix is

$$T = \begin{bmatrix} 1 & 0 & 0 & 0 \\ 0 & 1 & 0 & 0 \\ 0 & 0 & 1 & 0 \\ t_x & t_y & t_z & 1 \end{bmatrix}$$

The three rotation matrices are

$$R_z = \begin{bmatrix} \cos\phi & \sin\phi & 0 & 0 \\ -\sin\phi & \cos\phi & 0 & 0 \\ 0 & 0 & 1 & 0 \\ 0 & 0 & 0 & 1 \end{bmatrix}$$

$$R_x = \begin{bmatrix} 1 & 0 & 0 & 0 \\ 0 & \cos\phi & \sin\phi & 0 \\ 0 & -\sin\phi & \cos\phi & 1 \\ 0 & 0 & 0 & 1 \end{bmatrix}$$

$$R_y = \begin{bmatrix} \cos\phi & 0 & -\sin\phi & 0 \\ 0 & 1 & 0 & 0 \\ \sin\phi & 0 & \cos\phi & 0 \\ 0 & 0 & 0 & 1 \end{bmatrix}$$

Write a program that scales, translates, and rotates objects in three dimensions using matrix multiplication for all three operations.

Bibliography

Beatty, J. C., and K. S. Booth, *Tutorial: Computer Graphics*. IEEE, New York, 1984.

Dorn, W. S., and D. D. McCracken, *Numerical Methods with FORTRAN IV Case Studies*. New York: John Wiley & Sons, 1972.

Dyck, V. A., J. D. Lawson, J. A. Smith, R. J. Beach, *Computing, An Introduction to Structured Problem Solving Using PASCAL*. Reston, Virginia: Reston Publishing Company, 1982.

Foley, J. D., and A. Van Dam, *Fundamentals of Interactive Computer Graphics*. Reading, Mass: Addison-Wesley, 1984.

Rice, J. R., *Numerical Methods, Software, and Analysis*. New York: McGraw-Hill, 1983.

Strang, G., *Linear Algebra and its Applications*. New York: Academic Press, 1976.

1 2 3 4 5 6 7 8 9 0